THE PELICAN SHAKESPEARE

GENERAL EDITOR : ALFRED HARBAGE

AB25

THE TAMING OF THE SHREW

WILLIAM SHAKESPEARE

The Taming of
the Shrew

EDITED BY RICHARD HOSLEY

PENGUIN BOOKS

BALTIMORE · MARYLAND

CONTENTS

SHAKESPEARE AND HIS STAGE

William Shakespeare was christened in Holy Trinity Church, Stratford-on-Avon, April 26, 1564. His birth is traditionally assigned to April 23rd. He was the eldest of four boys and two girls who survived infancy in the family of John Shakespeare, glover and trader of Henley Street, and his wife Mary Arden, daughter of a small landowner of Wilmcote. In 1568 John was elected Bailiff (equivalent to Mayor) of Stratford, having already filled the minor municipal offices. The town maintained for the sons of the burgesses a free school, taught by a university graduate and offering preparation in Latin sufficient for university entrance; its early registers are lost, but there can be little doubt that Shakespeare received the formal part of his education in this school.

On November 27, 1582, a license was issued for the marriage of William Shakespeare (aged eighteen) and Ann Hathaway (aged twenty-six), and on May 26, 1583, their child Susanna was christened in Holy Trinity Church. The inference that the marriage was forced upon the youth is natural but not inevitable; betrothal was legally binding at the time, and was sometimes regarded as conferring conjugal rights. Two additional children of the marriage, the twins Hamnet and Judith, were christened on February 2, 1585. Meanwhile the prosperity of the elder Shakespeares had declined, and William was impelled to seek a career outside Stratford.

The tradition that he spent some time as a country teacher is old but unverifiable. Because of the absence of records his early twenties are called the "lost years," and only one thing about them is certain — that at least some of these years were spent in winning a place in the acting profession. He may have begun as a provincial trouper, but by 1592 he was established in London and prominent enough to be attacked. In a pamphlet of that year, *Groatsworth of Wit,* the ailing Robert Greene complained of the neglect which university writers like himself had suffered from actors, one of whom was daring to set up as a playwright:

> ... an upstart crow beautified with our feathers, that with his *Tiger's heart wrapt in a player's hide* supposes he is as well able to bombast out a blank verse as the best of you, and being an absolute Johannes-factotum, is in his own conceit the only Shake-scene in a country.

The pun on his name, and the parody of his line "O tiger's heart wrapt in a woman's hide" (*III Henry VI*), pointed clearly to Shakespeare. Some of his admirers protested, and Henry Chettle, the editor of Greene's pamphlet, saw fit to apologize:

> I am as sorry as if the original fault had been my fault, because myself have seen his demeanor no less civil than he excellent in the quality he professes. Besides divers of worship have reported his uprightness of dealing, which argues his honesty, and his facetious grace in writing that approves his art. (Prefatory epistle, *Kind Heart's Dream*)

The plague closed the London theatres for many months in 1593–94, denying the actors their livelihood. To this period belong Shakespeare's two narrative poems, *Venus and Adonis* and *Rape of Lucrece,* both dedicated to the Earl of Southampton. No doubt the poet was rewarded with a gift of money as usual in such cases, but he did no further dedicating and we have no reliable information on whether Southampton, or anyone else, became his regular patron. His sonnets, first mentioned in 1598 and published without his consent in 1609, are intimate without being explicitly autobiographical. They seem to commemorate the poet's friendship with an idealized youth, rivalry with a more favored poet, and love affair with a dark mistress; and his bitterness when the mistress betrays him in conjunction with the friend; but it is difficult to decide precisely what the "story" is, impossible to decide whether it is fictional or true. The real distinction of the sonnets, at least of those not purely conventional, rests in the universality of the thoughts and moods they express, and in their poignancy and beauty.

In 1594 was formed the theatrical company known until 1603 as the Lord Chamberlain's Men, thereafter as the King's Men. Its original membership included, besides Shakespeare, the beloved clown Will Kempe and the famous actor Richard Burbage. The company acted in various London theatres and even toured the provinces, but it is chiefly associated in our minds with the Globe Theatre built on the south bank of the Thames in 1599. Shakespeare was an actor and joint owner of this company (and its Globe) through the remainder of his creative years. His plays, written at the average rate of two a year, together with Burbage's acting won it its place of leadership among the London companies.

Individual plays began to appear in print, in editions both honest and piratical, and the publishers became increasingly aware of the value of Shakespeare's name on the title pages. As early as 1598 he was hailed as the leading English dramatist in the *Palladis Tamia* of Francis Meres:

As Plautus and Seneca are accounted the best for Comedy and Tragedy among the Latins, so Shakespeare among the English is the most excellent in both kinds for the stage: for Comedy, witness his *Gentlemen of Verona*, his *Errors*, his *Love labors lost*, his *Love labors won* [*Taming of the Shrew?*], his *Midsummers night dream*, & his *Merchant of Venice*; for Tragedy, his *Richard the 2*, *Richard the 3*, *Henry the 4*, *King John*, *Titus Andronicus*, and his *Romeo and Juliet*.

The note is valuable, both in indicating Shakespeare's prestige and in helping us to establish a chronology. In the second half of his writing career, history plays gave place to the great tragedies; and farces and light comedies gave place to the problem plays and symbolic romances. In 1623, seven years after his death, his former fellow actors, John Hemming and Henry Condell, cooperated with a group of London printers in bringing out his plays in collected form. The volume is generally known as the First Folio.

Shakespeare had never severed his relations with Stratford. His wife and children may sometimes have shared his London lodgings, but their home was Stratford. His son Hamnet was buried there in 1596, and his daughters Susanna and Judith were married there in 1607 and 1616 respectively. (His father, for whom he had secured a coat of arms and thus the privilege of writing himself gentleman, died in 1601, his mother in 1608.) His considerable earnings in London, as actor-sharer, part owner of the Globe, and playwright, were invested chiefly in Stratford property. In 1597 he purchased for £60 New Place, one of the two most imposing residences in the town. A number of other business transactions, as well as minor episodes in his career, have left documentary records. By 1611 he was in a position to retire, and he seems gradually to have withdrawn from theatrical activity in order to live in Stratford. In March, 1616, he made a will, leaving token bequests to Burbage, Hemming, and Condell, but the bulk of his estate to his family. The most famous feature of the will, the bequest of the second-best bed to his wife, reveals nothing about Shakespeare's marriage; the quaintness of the provision seems commonplace to those familiar with ancient testaments. Shakespeare died April 23, 1616, and was buried in the Stratford church where he had been christened. Within seven years a monument was erected to his memory on the north wall of the chancel. Its portrait bust and the Droeshout engraving on the title page of the First Folio provide the only likenesses with an established claim to authenticity. The best verbal vignette was written by his rival Ben Jonson, the more impressive for being imbedded in a context mainly critical:

> . . . I loved the man, and do honor his memory (on this side idolatry) as much as any. He was indeed honest, and of an open and free nature: he had an excellent fancy, brave notions, and gentle expressions. . . . (*Timber or Discoveries*, c. 1623–30)

The reader of Shakespeare's plays is aided by a general knowledge of the way in which they were staged. The King's Men acquired a roofed and artificially lighted theatre only toward the close of Shakespeare's career, and then only for winter use. Nearly all his plays were designed for performance in such structures as the Globe – a three-tiered amphitheatre with a large rectangular platform extending to the center of its yard. The plays were staged by daylight, by large casts brilliantly costumed, but with only a minimum of properties, without scenery, and quite possibly without intermissions. There was a rear stage balcony for action "above," and a curtained rear recess for "discoveries" and other special effects, but by far the major portion of any play was enacted upon the projecting platform, with episode following episode in swift succession, and with shifts of time and place signaled the audience only by the momentary clearing of the stage between the episodes. Information about the identity of the characters and, when necessary, about the time and place of the action was incorporated in the dialogue. No additional indications of place have been inserted in the present editions; these are apt to obscure the original fluidity of structure, with the emphasis upon action and speech rather than scenic background. The acting, including that of the youthful apprentices to the profession who performed the parts of women, was highly skillful, with a premium placed upon grace of gesture and beauty of diction. The audiences, a cross section of the general public, commonly numbered a thousand, sometimes more than two thousand. Judged by the type of plays they applauded, these audiences were not only large but also perceptive.

THE TEXTS OF THE PLAYS

About half of Shakespeare's plays appeared in print for the first time in the folio volume of 1623. The others had been published individually, usually in quarto volumes, during his lifetime or in the six years following his death. The copy used by the printers of the quartos varied greatly in merit, sometimes representing Shakespeare's true text, sometimes only a debased version of that text. The copy used by the printers of the folio also varied in merit, but was chosen with care. Since it consisted of the best available manuscripts, or the more acceptable quartos (although frequently in editions other than the first), or of quartos corrected by reference to manuscripts, we have good or reasonably good texts of most of the thirty-seven plays.

In the present series, the plays have been newly edited from quarto or folio texts depending, when a choice offered, upon which is now regarded by bibliographical specialists as the more authoritative. The ideal has been to reproduce the chosen texts with as few alterations as possible, beyond occasional relineation, expansion of abbreviations, and modernization of punctuation and spelling. Emendation is held to a minimum, and such material as has been added, in the way of stage directions and lines supplied by an alternative text, has been enclosed in square brackets.

None of the plays printed in Shakespeare's lifetime were divided into acts and scenes, and the inference is that the author's own manuscripts were not so divided. In the folio collection, some of the plays remained undivided, some were divided into acts, and some were divided into acts and scenes. During the eighteenth century all of the plays were divided into acts and scenes, and in the Cambridge edition of the mid-nineteenth century, from which the influential Globe text derived, this divison was more or less regularized and the lines were numbered. Many useful works of reference employ the act-scene-line apparatus established by the Globe text.

Since the act-scene division thus established is obviously convenient, but is of very dubious authority so far as Shakespeare's own structural principles are concerned, or the original manner of staging his plays, a problem is presented to modern editors. In the present series the act-scene division of the Globe text is retained marginally, and may be viewed as a reference aid like the line numbering. A printer's ornament marks the points of division when these points have been determined by a cleared stage indicating a shift of time and place in the action of the play, or when no harm results from the editorial assumption that there is such a shift. However, at those points where the established division is clearly misleading – that is, where continuous action has been split up into separate "scenes" – the ornament is omitted and the distortion corrected. This mechanical expedient seemed the best means of combining utility and accuracy.

The General Editor.

INTRODUCTION

Directors of *The Taming of the Shrew* corrupt its meaning when they bring Petruchio on stage cracking a whip. Admittedly such stage business would be appropriate to an extra-Shakespearean literary tradition, conspicuous in medieval *fabliaux* and Elizabethan jestbooks, according to which the husband of a shrewish wife forced her to mend her ways by beating her or otherwise subjecting her to physical cruelty. An example is the anonymous Elizabethan ballad, *A Merry Jest of a Shrewd and Curst Wife Lapped in Morel's Skin for Her Good Behavior* (printed about 1550). In this singularly unmerry tale a wife seeks frankly to dominate her husband. When she persists in shrewish behavior, he beats her with birch rods till the blood runs on the floor and she faints. He then wraps her in the skin of an old lame ploughhorse, Morel, killed and flayed especially for the occasion. Morel's salted skin quickly "revives" the wife, and the husband threatens to keep her in it unless she yields him mastership. At this "her mood begins to sink" and she promises obedience. She becomes an exemplary wife.

Shakespeare seems to have known this bit of Elizabethan Grand Guignol, for the basic situation of *The Taming of the Shrew* closely resembles that of the *Shrewd and Curst Wife*. However, he made no use whatever of the method of wife-taming recommended in that story. He accepted rather a humanist tradition, well represented by Erasmus in *A Merry Dialogue Declaring the Properties of Shrewd Wives and Honest Wives* (translation printed 1557), and by Vives in *The Office and Duty of an Husband* (translation printed about 1553). According to this tradition, the husband of a shrewish wife did not resort to violence, but led her, gently but firmly, to accept his rightful authority, much as he would teach a colt to go through its paces or a hawk to fly to the lure. Thus Petruchio "famishes" and "watches" his "haggard," Kate, but he always addresses her in courteous language and he never strikes her. The spanking he administers in most modern productions, like the whip he is made to carry, has no authority in the text of the play; it is a twentieth-century stage tradition, as the whip is a nineteenth-century one. The difficulty with these titillating sadistic touches, each perhaps innocent enough on the surface, is that they suggest, ultimately, a brutal domination of wife by husband. Accordingly Kate's speech on the subordination of wife to husband is sometimes misinterpreted as the blueprint for a husband's tyranny. Most spectators know better, despite what they are shown on the stage, for it is unlikely that *The Shrew* would be one of the most popular of Shakespeare's plays in the modern theatre if it really portrayed the subjugation of a wife through brutality. Incidentally, Kate's speech on subordination of the wife was probably, without denial of the basic validity of its doctrine, as susceptible to an ironic interpretation in Shakespeare's day as in our own. Vives, in *The Instruction of a Christian Woman* (translation printed 1540), quotes the wise saw, "A good woman by lowly obeisance ruleth her husband." Certainly the Elizabethans, in their view of the marriage relationship as of other things, were much more conscious of "degree" than we are:

Such duty as the subject owes the prince,
Even such a woman oweth to her husband;
And when she is froward, peevish, sullen, sour,
And not obedient to his honest will,
What is she but a foul contending rebel
And graceless traitor to her loving lord?

But they too could recognize the paradox that he who is ruled can also rule.

When we first see Kate, she is a spoiled household bully who tyrannizes over her sister and openly defies her father's authority. Without provocation she strikes her sister, her music-master, and her suitor. She is, in the terms of the play, shrewd, rough, sullen, headstrong, intolerable curst, stark mad or wonderful froward, impatient, angry, envious, revengeful, proud-minded, bent on pleasing herself, a wildcat, a chider, a railer, an irksome brawling scold, a devil, the devil's dam, a fiend of hell, and a hilding of a devilish spirit. In short, she is a shrew; and Petruchio, a husband for her turn, is the man born to tame her. But "taming" is only a metaphor. We can describe the action just as well by saying that Petruchio cures Kate of chronic bad temper. And he does so by employing a therapeutic method more in favor with the Elizabethans than with us, that of driving out poison with poison. He pretends to have the same sort of bad temper that she has, and he behaves with a wanton capriciousness that out-Kates Kate. Thus, more shrew than she, he kills her in her own humor; and thus, through him as through a mirror, Kate achieves self-knowledge. Petruchio's psychology is subtle, for, besides showing her what she is through his own outrageous behavior, he keeps telling her what she may become, praising her with a fine irony for qualities precisely the opposite of her defects. He speaks to her father of her affability and bashful modesty, her wondrous qualities and mild behavior; he praises her to her face as mild, gentle, pleasant, and passing courteous; and he compares her in patience to a second Grissel. The result is that when Kate is ready to modify her personality she has at hand a model on which to pattern herself. As the ugly old woman in the medieval romance changes after her marriage into a beautiful young one, so Katherine the curst changes, after her marriage, into a young woman of congenial and wholesome disposition. Or, to suggest another aspect of her psychic metamorphosis, she comes to accept the social relationship of wife to husband.

Although countless medieval and Renaissance stories deal with conflict between husband and wife, it is now generally agreed that there is no single extant source for the Petruchio-Kate story in its entirety. The *Shrewd and Curst Wife* is not usually regarded as a source, in part perhaps because its brutality is quickly recognized as foreign to Shakespeare's conception. But if we grant that an altogether different sort of "taming" is in question, it seems not unlikely that the anonymous ballad suggested the basic framework of Shakespeare's play. In the ballad, a man with a shrewish wife has two daughters. The younger is the father's favorite, meek and gentle, sought after by many suitors. The older is the mother's favorite, and like her a shrew; she is frantic, mad, without suitors. But finally a suitor appears who wishes to marry her. The father warns him against the shrewish daughter, likening her to "a devilish fiend of hell." The suitor says he sees no evil in her, marries her, and proceeds to "tame" her, by dint of birch rods and Morel's skin. At the close of the story the father, mother, and neighbors, entertained at a dinner, marvel at the wife's "good behavior." The tale ends with the jingle, "He that can charm a shrewd wife Better than thus, Let him come to me and fetch ten pound And a golden purse." All of these details but the shrewish mother and the brutal taming crop up, transmuted, in Shakespeare.

Other elements of Shakespeare's main plot have recognizable sources or analogues. The episode of rating a tailor for cutting a gown in fantastical fashion (IV, iii) occurs in Gerard Legh's *Accidence of Armory* (1562). The business of a wife's agreeing with her husband in his assertion of what is palpably not true (IV, v) occurs in *El Conde Lucanor* of Don Juan Manuel (around 1350). And the device of three husbands wagering on their wives' obedience (V, ii) occurs in *The Book of the Knight of La Tour-Landry* (translation printed 1484). None of these stories is necessarily a direct source of the corresponding episode in Shakespeare, but in each case the general similarity is such that we may suppose Shakespeare adapted an available tradition, incorporating his adaptation within a framework suggested by the *Shrewd and Curst Wife*.

Within this framework Shakespeare also incorporated a subplot based on George Gascoigne's *Supposes,* acted at Gray's Inn in 1566 and again at Trinity College, Oxford, in 1582. This is a fairly close translation of Lodovico Ariosto's *Suppositi,* acted at Ferrara in 1509, one of the earliest extant examples of Italian Renaissance comedy in the classical tradition represented by Menander, Plautus, and Terence. Ariosto's plot is fairly typical of the tradition: a young man succeeds in possessing the girl he loves by outwitting the character who blocks his access to her. In the Greco-Roman comedies the girl is usually a sort of junior courtesan, technically a slave and hence not marriageable; and the character guarding her from access is usually a pander or courtesan possessing legal title. Generally the young man's slave conducts the necessary intrigue, and if money is also needed, as it usually is, a second intrigue may be undertaken to swindle the young man's father. Sometimes the girl is pregnant, and sometimes it is discovered that she is a citizen, stolen as a baby by pirates or otherwise victimized by circumstance, in which case the play ends with the promise of marriage. Erostrato (Lucentio) as lover, Dulipo (Tranio) as the servant who conducts an intrigue in his young master's interest, and Philogano (Vincentio) as the father who is hoaxed by his son's servant – these characters Ariosto drew straight from classical comedy. But in his, as in similar Renaissance redactions, new character-types appeared reflecting altered social customs, along with new plots drawn from the medieval *novelle*. The core of the plot, and the character of the young man, remained much the same as in classical comedy, but the girl became either the wife or daughter of a citizen instead of the chattel of a courtesan or pander, and the character to be duped out of the girl became either a husband or father. Thus Ariosto's additional characters are "modern," no one quite like them appearing in surviving classical comedy: Polinesta (Bianca), a marriageable girl of wealthy family; Damon (Baptista), a rich father wishing to marry off a daughter; Balia (expunged by Shakespeare), a chaperon-nurse; and the rival suitors Cleander (Gremio) and Dulipo-the-supposed-Erostrato (Tranio-the-supposed-Lucentio).

Shakespeare modifies these received character-types, two of them in particular. Lucentio is quite different from the young man of classical comedy or from Erostrato in the *Supposes*, for he not only wishes to marry the girl but also has no intention of seducing her. He represents a romantic tradition, that of the chaste wooer or rapturous lover. Bianca is even further from classical comedy than Polinesta, for she also represents a romantic tradition, that of the chaste heroine who can be possessed only in marriage. Not being promiscuous, she has no need of a go-between; and hence Shakespeare does not need a character corresponding to Balia. Thus he shifts the emphasis from sexual intrigue to winning the girl's hand in marriage, omitting both Polinesta's pregnancy and the slightly grim episode of the outraged father's imprisoning his daughter's lover. The character of Hortensio is a significant innovation, for in the *Supposes* the disguised lover has no competitor. Thus Shakespeare provides two *sub rosa* suitors (Lucentio and Hortensio) who appeal directly to the girl, in addition to the two open suitors (Tranio and Gremio) who appeal to the girl's father. Lucentio therefore has a potentially effective rival, and Bianca exercises choice. Though subjected to gentle mockery, Hortensio has a sympathetic character. Accordingly he must be matched with a wife at the end, and so the Widow is dragged in as a sort of *madonna ex machina*. If we expect realism this last-minute mating may seem awkward, but it is inevitable if the play is to end, as by convention a comedy should, in marriage for all the lovers, and if a genuine rivalry for the heroine is to be suggested, however briefly.

Since the *Supposes* has a "crisis" plot, with absolute unity of time and place, an important structural change is Shakespeare's adapting the story from the retrospective to the progressive mode of drama. He shows as successively occurring what Ariosto merely reports as having already occurred: the young man's falling in love with the girl upon seeing her in the street, his taking service in her father's household, his successful wooing. Another important structural change is the addition of a "stolen marriage" while the girl's father is negotiating with the fake suitor. From the point of view of plot there is a redundancy here, for Hortensio's rivalry is no longer a factor and the arrival of the lover's true father, as in the source, makes it possible, after exposure of Tranio and the fake father, for Lucentio to marry the girl – but he has taken the bit in his teeth and already married her! The point, of course, is that in proper romantic drama the lovers should effect their own marriage, without regard for the wishes of their elders. Shakespeare employed the device of a stolen marriage more effectively in *Romeo and Juliet* and *The Merry Wives of Windsor,* in each of which a stolen marriage is the only alternative to the girl's being forced to marry an undesirable suitor favored by her parents.

Shakespeare's dramaturgical skill is especially evident in his welding of two parallel actions, the construction bearing comparison with that of *The Merchant of Venice* or *Much Ado about Nothing.* A few loose ends and minor flaws in the plotting do not affect the general truth of Dr. Johnson's criticism: "Of this play the two plots are so well united, that they can hardly be called two without injury to the art with which they are interwoven." Since the subplot involves only wooing and marriage, it proceeds at a slower pace than the main plot, which involves wooing, marriage, and the "taming." Throughout the first three acts the two plots run together in parallel, tightly linked by the father's insistence that the elder daughter be wed before the younger. Lucentio falls in love with Bianca (I, i), Tranio and Gremio sue to Baptista for her hand in marriage (II, i), and Lucentio and Hortensio woo her in disguise (III, i). Petruchio decides to marry Kate (I, ii), woos her (II, i), and marries her (III, ii). In the fourth act the two stories diverge. The subplot, after enlistment of the Pedant (IV, ii), forks into the gulling of Baptista and the planning of the stolen marriage (IV, iv). The main plot pursues the "taming" through the episodes of the burnt meat (IV, i) and the Tailor (IV, iii) to the meeting of Petruchio and Kate with Vincentio (IV, v). At this point the two stories, loosely connected by Hortensio's appearance in the main plot (IV, iii) after his dismissal from the subplot (IV, ii), are again united. The denouement of the "taming" action occurs in IV, v, when Kate accepts the sun as the moon and Vincentio as a young woman. This episode neatly prepares us for the denial of Vincentio's identity in V, i. The denouement of the "supposes" action occurs in this scene, with the exposure of Tranio's hoax and the reappearance of the runaway lovers as husband and wife. Technically anticlimactic, the last scene (V, ii) emphasizes the unity of the two actions by suggesting, through an exhibition of Kate's reformed nature, that Bianca and the Widow are shrews under the skin. This scene gives us also, in Lucentio's banquet, an effective symbol of the "new" society which normally "crystallizes" around the lovers when they marry at the end of a comedy.

To the parallel actions of *The Taming of the Shrew* Shakespeare added, in the form of an "induction," a third action, the gulling of Christopher Sly. This much admired sequence of comedy is an example of a widespread motif originating in the story of "The Sleeper Awakened" in *The Arabian Nights*. Early in the sixteenth century the story was retold by Vives as having actually occurred in Brussels around 1440, with Philip the Good, Duke of Burgundy, in the role of Shakespeare's Lord. Much the same version was recounted by Heuterus in *De rebus burgundicis* (1584). Up to a point, the story in Heuterus, if we allow for variations between prose fiction and verse drama, is generally similar to that in Shakespeare. The chief difference is that the deluded artisan who corresponds to Shakespeare's Sly, having fallen asleep after a banquet, is once again dressed in his rags and returned to the street where he had been found in a drunken sleep the night before; in the morning he imagines he has dreamt what happened to him. The difficult question therefore arises whether Shakespeare concluded Sly's story with a "dramatic epilogue" which for some reason was omitted from the printed text, or whether he intended his "presenters" to disappear unobtrusively after their short "interlude" at the end of I, i. A conclusive answer may not be possible. In support of the first interpretation it can be argued that Shakespeare would not have left the Sly story up in the air after so brilliant a beginning, and that the story is "finished" in all other versions, including a dramatic one, *The Taming of a Shrew,* in some manner related to Shakespeare's play (cf. Appendix). In support of the second interpretation it can be argued that Shakespeare would have tended to avoid a dramatic epilogue as anticlimactic, that its omission would have harmonized with the Elizabethan theatrical practice of doubling roles of the induction with roles of the play proper (thus making it awkward for actors on stage at the end of the play to return to their roles of the induction), and that the thematic statement of Shakespeare's Sly material is complete as we have it – Sly's story is in effect "finished" when, like Kate, he has been persuaded to accept a new personality.

In any case, the action of Shakespeare's induction is as closely related to the parallel actions of his play proper as each of those actions is to the other – except that where the double relationship is explicit, in terms chiefly of plot, the triple one is implicit, in terms chiefly of theme. Taken together, the three actions constitute a complex of compared and contrasted poses and "supposes" – Gascoigne's word for Ariosto's *suppositi*, i.e. "assumptions." The Lord-Sly action is concerned with assumptions about identity and with how these can lead to assumptions about personality. The Lord poses as a servant and, with the aid of his servants, induces Sly to suppose himself a lord. The Lord's page poses as Sly's wife. The Petruchio-Kate action is concerned mainly with assumptions about personality, partly with assumptions about identity. Is Kate's shrewishness a pose? At any rate, Petruchio poses as a male shrew and induces Kate to accept his "supposition" that she is not a shrew but a modest and civil young woman. Together Kate and Petruchio pretend to suppose that Vincentio is a young woman. And the Lucentio-Bianca action is concerned mainly with assumptions about identity, partly with assumptions about personality. Lucentio poses as a schoolmaster, Hortensio as a music-master. Tranio poses as Lucentio, induces the Pedant to pose as Vincentio, and pretends to suppose that Vincentio is not himself – in fact, that he is a poseur. Gremio the pantaloon supposes himself a lover. Bianca and the Widow pose as models of female behavior, and Lucentio and Hortensio mistakenly suppose that their wives are obedient.

The foregoing discussion emphasizes the architectonic skill with which the component parts of *The Taming of the Shrew* were combined to make an esthetically effective whole. That Shakespeare was the sole author of the play is now generally granted, but whether it was he who originally conceived its threefold structure is a question still open to debate. According to a view held by some scholars, Shakespeare may have used as a source a lost play consisting of the main outlines of his three interconnected actions. One may feel skeptical about this theory of a "lost original," in part because there is no historical evidence for the existence of such a play (as there is in the case of *Hamlet*), in part because the theory is only a postulate to account for the relations between Shakespeare's play and the extant *Taming of a Shrew*, an anonymous text printed in 1594. At present the probability seems to be that *A Shrew* is neither Shakespeare's source nor a version of some lost original play, but an imitation of *The Taming of the Shrew* itself (cf. Appendix). It is doubtful whether by 1594 any English dramatist other than Shakespeare was sufficiently skilled in plot-construction to write such a carefully and subtly integrated triple-action play as we should have to suppose a lost original to be if *A Shrew* were derived from it in the manner envisaged by modern textual theory.

Structural integrity and thematic unity are important aspects of the artistic excellence of *The Taming of the Shrew*. But since these qualities often go unnoticed, neither can be counted as the chief reason for the play's enduring popularity. It is a curious fact that the play rates higher with directors, actors, and spectators than it does with critics, teachers, and readers. One reason for this may be that *The Shrew* is much funnier in performance than it is on the printed page. The fun derives from many sources — for example, Sly's wary acceptance of his preposterous situation, the delicate comedy of the undercover wooing of Bianca, Biondello's grotesque catalogue of equine ailments, the farcical business of the burnt meat, Kate's bewilderment at Petruchio's zany behavior, the efforts of the Tailor to control himself, the comic irony of the confrontation of Vincentio with the Pedant. But perhaps the chief reason for the appeal of the play is the vivid characterization of

Sly, Petruchio, and Kate — the most memorable of Shakespeare's creations before Juliet, Mercutio, and the Nurse. These parts, when animated by good actors, can charm an audience utterly. They have this power not only because of Shakespeare's comic genius but also because of the truth to human nature which he has woven into his language. To a degree, each of us who engages in the War between the Sexes must cope with the sort of problem faced by Petruchio or Kate. Like other of Shakespeare's plays, *The Taming of the Shrew* deals with an archetypal situation.

University of Arizona   RICHARD HOSLEY

Note on the text: This edition follows the text of the Shakespeare folio of 1623, thought to have been printed from a Shakespearean manuscript. Significant emendations are listed in the Appendix. The folio text is not divided into scenes, and its act-division is unsatisfactory. In F, Induction i is labeled I, i, Acts I and II are not indicated, and Acts III, IV, and V begin, respectively, at III, i, IV, iii, and V, ii of the act-scene division of the Globe text, which is supplied marginally in the present edition.

The Taming of the Shrew

[Names of the Actors

In the Induction

A Lord, later posing as a servant
Christopher Sly
Bartholomew, page to the Lord, posing as Sly's wife
A company of strolling Players
Huntsmen and Servants to the Lord
Hostess of a tavern

In the Play Proper

Baptista Minola, father to Kate and Bianca
Vincentio, father to Lucentio
Gremio, a pantaloon, suitor to Bianca
Lucentio, in love with Bianca, later posing as Cambio
Hortensio, suitor to Bianca, later posing as Litio
Petruchio, suitor to Kate
A Pedant, later posing as Vincentio
Tranio, servant to Lucentio, later posing as Lucentio
Biondello, page to Lucentio
Grumio, servant to Petruchio
Curtis, servant to Petruchio
A Tailor
A Haberdasher
Katherine (Kate), the Shrew
Bianca
A Widow
Servants to Baptista, Petruchio, Lucentio

Scene
Warwickshire; Padua; near Verona]

THE TAMING OF THE SHREW

Enter Beggar (Christophero Sly) and Hostess.

Sly. I'll feeze you, in faith.

Hostess. A pair of stocks, you rogue!

Sly. Y'are a baggage, the Slys are no rogues. Look in the chronicles: we came in with Richard Conqueror. Therefore paucas pallabris, let the world slide. Sessa! 5

Hostess. You will not pay for the glasses you have burst?

Sly. No, not a denier. Go by, St. Jeronimy, go to thy cold bed and warm thee.

Hostess. I know my remedy: I must go fetch the thirdborough. *[Exit.]* 10

Sly. Third or fourth or fifth borough, I'll answer him by law. I'll not budge an inch, boy: let him come, and kindly. *Falls asleep.*

Ind., i, 1 *feeze you* settle your hash 2 *A pair of stocks* (she threatens him with punishment) 4 *Richard* (Sly's mistake for William) 5 *paucas pallabris* i.e. pocas palabras, few words (Spanish) *Sessa* (interjection of doubtful meaning) 7 *denier* copper coin of small value *Go by, St. Jeronimy* (Sly's version of a stock phrase expressing impatience, from Kyd's *Spanish Tragedy*) 9–10 *thirdborough* constable (*third*, which Sly mistakes for the number, derives from the old word *frith*, peace)

Wind horns. Enter a Lord from hunting, with his
Train.

Lord. Huntsman, I charge thee, tender well my hounds.
15 Breathe Merriman, the poor cur is embossed,
And couple Clowder with the deep-mouthed brach.
Saw'st thou not, boy, how Silver made it good
At the hedge-corner in the coldest fault?
I would not lose the dog for twenty pound.
20 *1. Huntsman.* Why Bellman is as good as he, my lord.
He cried upon it at the merest loss
And twice to-day picked out the dullest scent.
Trust me, I take him for the better dog.
Lord. Thou art a fool. If Echo were as fleet,
25 I would esteem him worth a dozen such.
But sup them well and look unto them all.
To-morrow I intend to hunt again.
1. Huntsman. I will, my lord.
Lord. What's here? One dead or drunk? See, doth he
breathe?
2. Huntsman. He breathes, my lord. Were he not warmed
30 with ale
This were a bed but cold to sleep so soundly.
Lord. O monstrous beast, how like a swine he lies!
Grim death, how foul and loathsome is thine image!
Sirs, I will practice on this drunken man.
35 What think you, if he were conveyed to bed,
Wrapped in sweet clothes, rings put upon his fingers,
A most delicious banquet by his bed,

---

13 S.D. *Wind* sound   14 *tender* care for   15 *Breathe* rest   *embossed* foaming at the mouth   16 *brach* bitch-hound   18 *fault* loss of scent   21 *cried* gave tongue   *at the merest loss* when the scent was totally lost   34 *practice* play a trick   36 *sweet* perfumed

And brave attendants near him when he wakes,
Would not the beggar then forget himself?
1. Huntsman. Believe me, lord, I think he cannot choose. 40
2. Huntsman. It would seem strange unto him when he
    waked.
Lord. Even as a flatt'ring dream or worthless fancy.
    Then take him up and manage well the jest.
    Carry him gently to my fairest chamber
    And hang it round with all my wanton pictures.   45
    Balm his foul head in warm distillèd waters
    And burn sweet wood to make the lodging sweet.
    Procure me music ready when he wakes
    To make a dulcet and a heavenly sound.
    And if he chance to speak be ready straight,   50
    And with a low submissive reverence
    Say, 'What is it your honor will command?'
    Let one attend him with a silver basin
    Full of rose-water and bestrewed with flowers,
    Another bear the ewer, the third a diaper,   55
    And say, 'Will't please your lordship cool your hands?'
    Some one be ready with a costly suit
    And ask him what apparel he will wear,
    Another tell him of his hounds and horse
    And that his lady mourns at his disease.   60
    Persuade him that he hath been lunatic,
    And when he says he is, say that he dreams,
    For he is nothing but a mighty lord.
    This do, and do it kindly, gentle sirs.
    It will be pastime passing excellent,   65
    If it be husbanded with modesty.

38 *brave* finely dressed   46 *Balm* anoint   50 *straight* immediately   55 *dia-per* linen towel   62 *is* i.e. lunatic   64 *kindly* naturally   65 *passing* surpassingly   66 *husbanded* managed   *modesty* moderation

1. Huntsman. My lord, I warrant you we will play our part,
      As he shall think, by our true diligence,
      He is no less than what we say he is.
70 *Lord.* Take him up gently, and to bed with him,
      And each one to his office when he wakes.
                    [Sly is carried out.] Sound trumpets.
      Sirrah, go see what trumpet 'tis that sounds.
                              [Exit Servingman.]
      Belike some noble gentleman that means,
      Travelling some journey, to repose him here.

                    Enter Servingman.

75   How now, who is it?
Servingman. An't please your honor, players
      That offer service to your lordship.

                    Enter Players.

Lord. Bid them come near.— Now, fellows, you are
      welcome.
Players. We thank your honor.
80 *Lord.* Do you intend to stay with me to-night?
A Player. So please your lordship to accept our duty.
Lord. With all my heart. This fellow I remember
      Since once he played a farmer's eldest son.
      'Twas where you wooed the gentlewoman so well.
85   I have forgot your name, but sure that part
      Was aptly fitted and naturally performed.
A Player. I think 'twas Soto that your honor means.
Lord. 'Tis very true, thou didst it excellent.
      Well, you are come to me in happy time,
90   The rather for I have some sport in hand

68 *As* so that   72 *Sirrah* (usual form of address to an inferior)   73 *Belike*
probably   76 *An* if   81 *duty* expression of respect   89 *happy* opportune

Wherein your cunning can assist me much.
There is a lord will hear you play to-night –
But I am doubtful of your modesties,
Lest, over-eyeing of his odd behavior –
For yet his honor never heard a play –   95
You break into some merry passion
And so offend him; for I tell you, sirs,
If you should smile he grows impatient.
A Player. Fear not, my lord, we can contain ourselves
Were he the veriest antic in the world.   100
Lord. Go, sirrah, take them to the buttery
And give them friendly welcome every one.
Let them want nothing that my house affords.

                    Exit one with the Players.

Sirrah, go you to Barthol'mew my page
And see him dressed in all suits like a lady.   105
That done, conduct him to the drunkard's chamber
And call him madam; do him obeisance.
Tell him from me – as he will win my love –
He bear himself with honorable action
Such as he hath observed in noble ladies   110
Unto their lords, by them accomplishèd:
Such duty to the drunkard let him do
With soft low tongue and lowly courtesy,
And say, 'What is't your honor will command
Wherein your lady and your humble wife   115
May show her duty and make known her love?'
And then with kind embracements, tempting kisses,
And with declining head into his bosom,
Bid him shed tears, as being overjoyed

91 *cunning* skill   93 *modesties* discretion   94 *over-eyeing of* witnessing
96 *merry passion* fit of laughter   100 *antic* buffoon   101 *buttery* room
where liquor is kept   105 *suits* points

120   To see her noble lord restored to health
       Who for this seven years hath esteemèd him
       No better than a poor and loathsome beggar.
       And if the boy have not a woman's gift
       To rain a shower of commanded tears,

125   An onion will do well for such a shift,
       Which in a napkin being close conveyed
       Shall in despite enforce a watery eye.
       See this dispatched with all the haste thou canst:
       Anon I'll give thee more instructions.

                                        Exit a Servingman.

130   I know the boy will well usurp the grace,
       Voice, gait, and action of a gentlewoman.
       I long to hear him call the drunkard husband,
       And how my men will stay themselves from laughter
       When they do homage to this simple peasant.

135   I'll in to counsel them: haply my presence
       May well abate the over-merry spleen
       Which otherwise would grow into extremes.

                                             [Exeunt.]

Ind., ii   *Enter aloft the Drunkard [Sly] with Attendants, some with*
            apparel, basin and ewer, and other appurtenances; and
            Lord [as a Servant].

Sly. For God's sake! a pot of small ale.

121 *this seven years* (proverbial for an indefinitely long period)   *him* himself 125 *shift* purpose 126 *napkin* handkerchief   *close* secretly 129 *Anon*
right away 130 *usurp* assume 136 *spleen* mood Ind., ii s.d. *aloft* i.e.
in the tiring-house gallery over the stage (Capell, 1768, supplied a stage
direction calling for a bed and other stage properties, but l. 35 makes
clear that a bed was not used in the original staging) 1 *small* weak
(hence cheap)

1. Servingman. Will't please your lordship drink a cup of
    sack?

2. Servingman. Will't please your honor taste of these
    conserves?

3. Servingman. What raiment will your honor wear to-day?

Sly. I am Christophero Sly, call not me honor nor lord- 5
    ship. I ne'er drank sack in my life, and if you give me any
    conserves, give me conserves of beef. Ne'er ask me what
    raiment I'll wear, for I have no more doublets than backs,
    no more stockings than legs, nor no more shoes than
    feet; nay, sometime more feet than shoes, or such shoes 10
    as my toes look through the overleather.

Lord. Heaven cease this idle humor in your honor!
    O that a mighty man of such descent,
    Of such possessions and so high esteem,
    Should be infusèd with so foul a spirit! 15

Sly. What, would you make me mad? Am not I Chris-
    topher Sly, old Sly's son of Burton-heath, by birth
    a pedlar, by education a cardmaker, by transmutation a
    bearherd, and now by present profession a tinker? Ask
    Marian Hacket, the fat ale-wife of Wincot, if she know 20
    me not. If she say I am not fourteen pence on the score
    for sheer ale, score me up for the lyingest knave in
    Christendom. What, I am not bestraught: here's —

3. Servingman. O this it is that makes your lady mourn.

2. Servingman. O this it is that makes your servants droop. 25

2 *sack* sherry (a gentleman's drink)   3 *conserves* candied fruit   7 *conserves
of beef* salt beef   8 *doublets* coats   12 *humor* obsession   17 *Burton-heath*
Barton-on-the-Heath (a village some fifteen miles south of Stratford)
18 *cardmaker* (a card was a comb used in preparing wool for spinning)
19 *bearherd* keeper of a tame bear   *tinker* itinerant pot-mender (proverbially
a hard drinker)   20 *Wincot* a hamlet some four miles southwest of Stratford (Hackets were living in the parish in 1591)   21 *on the score* chalked
up as owing   22 *sheer* unmixed   *score me up for* write me down as   23
bestraught distraught, mad

Lord. Hence comes it that your kindred shuns your
　　house,
　　As beaten hence by your strange lunacy.
　　O noble lord, bethink thee of thy birth,
　　Call home thy ancient thoughts from banishment
30　And banish hence these abject lowly dreams.
　　Look how thy servants do attend on thee,
　　Each in his office ready at thy beck.
　　Wilt thou have music? Hark, Apollo plays,　　*Music.*
　　And twenty cagèd nightingales do sing.
35　Or wilt thou sleep? We'll have thee to a couch
　　Softer and sweeter than the lustful bed
　　On purpose trimmed up for Semiramis.
　　Say thou wilt walk, we will bestrew the ground.
　　Or wilt thou ride? Thy horses shall be trapped,
40　Their harness studded all with gold and pearl.
　　Dost thou love hawking? Thou hast hawks will soar
　　Above the morning lark. Or wilt thou hunt?
　　Thy hounds shall make the welkin answer them
　　And fetch shrill echoes from the hollow earth.
1. Servingman. Say thou wilt course, thy greyhounds are as
45　　swift
　　As breathèd stags, ay, fleeter than the roe.
2. Servingman. Dost thou love pictures? We will fetch thee
　　　straight
　　Adonis painted by a running brook
　　And Cytherea all in sedges hid,

29 *ancient* former　33 *Apollo* god of music　37 *Semiramis* legendary
lustful queen of Assyria　38 *bestrew* spread carpets on　39 *trapped* adorned
43 *welkin* sky　45 *course* hunt the hare with greyhounds　46 *breathèd* in
good wind　*roe* a kind of small deer　48 *Adonis* (loved by Venus and
killed by a wild boar while hunting; cf. Shakespeare's *Venus and Adonis*)
49 *Cytherea* Venus (associated with the island of Cythera)　*sedges* water-
rushes

38

Which seem to move and wanton with her breath   50
Even as the waving sedges play with wind.
Lord. We'll show thee Io as she was a maid
And how she was beguilèd and surprised,
As lively painted as the deed was done.
3. Servingman. Or Daphne roaming through a thorny
    wood,   55
Scratching her legs that one shall swear she bleeds,
And at that sight shall sad Apollo weep,
So workmanly the blood and tears are drawn.
Lord. Thou art a lord and nothing but a lord.
Thou hast a lady far more beautiful   60
Than any woman in this waning age.
1. Servingman. And till the tears that she hath shed for thee
Like envious floods o'er-run her lovely face
She was the fairest creature in the world,
And yet she is inferior to none.   65
Sly. Am I a lord, and have I such a lady?
Or do I dream? Or have I dreamed till now?
I do not sleep: I see, I hear, I speak,
I smell sweet savors and I feel soft things.
Upon my life, I am a lord indeed,   70
And not a tinker nor Christophero Sly.
Well, bring our lady hither to our sight,
And once again, a pot o' th' smallest ale.
2. Servingman. Will't please your mightiness to wash your
    hands?
O how we joy to see your wit restored!   75

---

50 *wanton* sway seductively   52 *Io* (loved by Jupiter in the shape of a cloud
and changed by him into a heifer to deceive the jealous Juno)   54 *lively*
realistically   55 *Daphne* (wooed by Apollo and changed into a laurel tree
to escape his pursuit)   61 *waning* degenerate   63 *envious* hateful   65 *yet*
even now   73 *smallest* weakest   75 *wit* reason

O that once more you knew but what you are!
These fifteen years you have been in a dream,
Or when you waked, so waked as if you slept.
Sly. These fifteen years? By my fay, a goodly nap.
80   But did I never speak of all that time?
1. Servingman. O yes, my lord, but very idle words,
For though you lay here in this goodly chamber,
Yet would you say ye were beaten out of door
And rail upon the hostess of the house,
85   And say you would present her at the leet
Because she brought stone jugs and no sealed quarts.
Sometimes you would call out for Cicely Hacket.
Sly. Ay, the woman's maid of the house.
3. Servingman. Why, sir, you know no house nor no such
        maid,
90   Nor no such men as you have reckoned up,
As Stephen Sly, and old John Naps of Greet,
And Peter Turph, and Henry Pimpernell,
And twenty more such names and men as these,
Which never were nor no man ever saw.
95 *Sly.* Now Lord be thankèd for my good amends!
All. Amen.

        Enter [the Page as a] Lady, with Attendants.

Sly. I thank thee, thou shalt not lose by it.
Page. How fares my noble lord?
Sly. Marry, I fare well, for here is cheer enough.
100   Where is my wife?

79 *fay* faith   84 *house* inn   85 *present* accuse   *leet* manorial court   86 *sealed* bearing an official seal indicating capacity   91 *Stephen Sly* (name of a Stratford citizen of Shakespeare's day)   *Greet* a hamlet near Winchcomb, about twenty miles southwest of Stratford   95 *amends* recovery   99 *Marry* indeed (originally an oath by the Virgin Mary)   *cheer* entertainment

Page. Here, noble lord, what is thy will with her?
Sly. Are you my wife and will not call me husband?
  My men should call me lord; I am your goodman.
Page. My husband and my lord, my lord and husband,
  I am your wife in all obedience.   105
Sly. I know it well. What must I call her?
Lord. Madam.
Sly. Al'ce madam or Joan madam?
Lord. Madam and nothing else, so lords call ladies.
Sly. Madam wife, they say that I have dreamed   110
  And slept above some fifteen year or more.
Page. Ay, and the time seems thirty unto me,
  Being all this time abandoned from your bed.
Sly. 'Tis much. Servants, leave me and her alone.
                              [Exeunt Servants.]
  Madam, undress you and come now to bed.   115
Page. Thrice noble lord, let me entreat of you
  To pardon me yet for a night or two,
  Or if not so, until the sun be set.
  For your physicians have expressly charged,
  In peril to incur your former malady,   120
  That I should yet absent me from your bed.
  I hope this reason stands for my excuse.
Sly. Ay, it stands so that I may hardly tarry so long – but
  I would be loath to fall into my dreams again. I will
  therefore tarry in despite of the flesh and the blood.   125

Enter a Messenger.

Messenger. Your honor's players, hearing your amendment,
  Are come to play a pleasant comedy,

103 *goodman* husband (a term that might be used by the wife of a yeoman
or husbandman) 113 *abandoned* banished 123 *it stands so* the case is
(with a bawdy quibble)

41

For so your doctors hold it very meet,
Seeing too much sadness hath congealed your **blood**
130   And melancholy is the nurse of frenzy.
Therefore they thought it good you hear a play
And frame your mind to mirth and merriment,
Which bars a thousand harms and lengthens life.

Sly. Marry, I will, let them play it. Is not a commonty **a**
135   Christmas gambol or a tumbling-trick?

Page. No, my good lord, it is more pleasing stuff.

Sly. What, household stuff?

Page. It is a kind of history.

Sly. Well, we'll see't. Come, madam wife, sit by my side
140   and let the world slip: we shall ne'er be younger.

[They sit over the stage.]

I, i   *Flourish. Enter [below] Lucentio and his man Tranio.*

Lucentio. Tranio, since for the great desire I had
To see fair Padua, nursery of arts,
I am arrived for fruitful Lombardy,
The pleasant garden of great Italy,
5   And by my father's love and leave am armed
With his good will and thy good company,
My trusty servant, well approved in all,
Here let us breathe and haply institute
A course of learning and ingenious studies.
10   Pisa, renownèd for grave citizens,
Gave me my being and my father first,

130 *frenzy* madness   134 *commonty* (Sly's mistake for 'comedy')   138
history story   I, i s.d. *man* servant   *Tranio* (name from the *Mostellaria* of
Plautus connoting 'clarifier, revealer')   2 *Padua* (famous for its university)   3 *Lombardy* northern Italy   7 *approved* i.e. proved dependable
9 *ingenious* intellectual   11 *first* i.e. before me

A merchant of great traffic through the world,
Vincentio, come of the Bentivolii.
Vincentio's son, brought up in Florence,
It shall become to serve all hopes conceived,   15
To deck his fortune with his virtuous deeds.
And therefore, Tranio, for the time I study
Virtue, and that part of philosophy
Will I apply that treats of happiness
By virtue specially to be achieved.   20
Tell me thy mind, for I have Pisa left
And am to Padua come, as he that leaves
A shallow plash to plunge him in the deep
And with satiety seeks to quench his thirst.
Tranio. Mi perdonato, gentle master mine.   25
I am in all affected as yourself,
Glad that you thus continue your resolve
To suck the sweets of sweet philosophy.
Only, good master, while we do admire
This virtue and this moral discipline,   30
Let's be no stoics nor no stocks, I pray,
Or so devote to Aristotle's checks
As Ovid be an outcast quite abjured.
Balk logic with acquaintance that you have
And practice rhetoric in your common talk.   35
Music and poesy use to quicken you.
The mathematics and the metaphysics,
Fall to them as you find your stomach serves you.

---

15 *serve* fulfill   19 *apply* pursue   23 *plash* pool   25 *Mi perdonato* pardon
me   26 *affected* inclined   31 *stocks* posts (i.e. incapable of feeling, punning
on *stoics*)   32 *checks* restraints   33 *Ovid* the Roman love poet (cf.
III, i, 28–29; IV, ii, 8)   *abjured* sworn off   34 *Balk logic* bandy arguments
36 *quicken* enliven   38 *stomach* appetite

No profit grows where is no pleasure ta'en.
40   In brief, sir, study what you most affect.
Lucentio. Gramercies, Tranio, well dost thou advise.
If, Biondello, thou wert come ashore,
We could at once put us in readiness
And take a lodging fit to entertain
45   Such friends as time in Padua shall beget.
But stay awhile, what company is this?
Tranio. Master, some show to welcome us to town.

Enter Baptista with his two daughters Kate and Bianca,
    Gremio a pantaloon, [and] Hortensio suitor to Bianca.
    Lucentio [and] Tranio stand by.

Baptista. Gentlemen, importune me no further,
For how I firmly am resolved you know.
50   That is, not to bestow my youngest daughter
Before I have a husband for the elder.
If either of you both love Katherina,
Because I know you well and love you well,
Leave shall you have to court her at your pleasure.
55 *Gremio.* To cart her rather, she's too rough for me.
There, there, Hortensio, will you any wife?
Kate. I pray you, sir, is it your will
To make a stale of me amongst these mates?
Hortensio. 'Mates,' maid, how mean you that? No mates
    for you

40 *affect* like 41 *Gramercies* many thanks 42 *come ashore* (Padua, like
Mantua and Bergamo later, is conceived of conventionally as a seaport)
47 S.D. *pantaloon* foolish old man (stock character of the *commedia del-
l'arte*) 55 *cart her* i.e. have her driven through the streets in a cart, like a
prostitute undergoing punishment 58 *stale* laughing-stock (playing on
'strumpet,' suggested by *cart*) *mates* low fellows (Hortensio quibbles
on 'husbands')

Unless you were of gentler, milder mold.   60
Kate. I' faith, sir, you shall never need to fear:
  Iwis it is not halfway to her heart.
  But if it were, doubt not her care should be
  To comb your noddle with a three-legged stool
  And paint your face and use you like a fool.   65
Hortensio. From all such devils, good Lord deliver us.
Gremio. And me too, good Lord.
Tranio. [*aside*] Hush, master, here's some good pastime
  toward.
  That wench is stark mad or wonderful froward.
Lucentio. But in the other's silence do I see   70
  Maid's mild behavior and sobriety.
  Peace, Tranio!
Tranio. Well said, master; mum, and gaze your fill.
Baptista. Gentlemen, that I may soon make good
  What I have said — Bianca, get you in,   75
  And let it not displease thee, good Bianca,
  For I will love thee ne'er the less, my girl.
Kate. A pretty peat! it is best
  Put finger in the eye, an she knew why.
Bianca. Sister, content you in my discontent.   80
  Sir, to your pleasure humbly I subscribe.
  My books and instruments shall be my company,
  On them to look and practice by myself.
Lucentio. [*aside*] Hark, Tranio, thou mayst hear Minerva
  speak.

---

60 *mold* character 62 *Iwis* indeed *it* i.e. marriage *her* i.e. Kate's 65
paint i.e. by drawing blood 68 *toward* in prospect 69 *froward* refractory
78 *peat* spoiled darling 79 *Put finger in the eye* i.e. weep *an* if 84
Minerva goddess of wisdom and of the arts

85 *Hortensio.* Signior Baptista, will you be so strange?
      Sorry am I that our good will effects
      Bianca's grief.
      Gremio.   Why, will you mew her up,
      Signior Baptista, for this fiend of hell
      And make her bear the penance of her tongue?
90 *Baptista.* Gentlemen, content ye, I am resolved.
      Go in, Bianca.   *[Exit Bianca.]*
      And for I know she taketh most delight
      In music, instruments, and poetry,
      Schoolmasters will I keep within my house,
95   Fit to instruct her youth. If you, Hortensio,
      Or Signior Gremio, you, know any such,
      Prefer them hither, for to cunning men
      I will be very kind, and liberal
      To mine own children in good bringing-up.
100 And so, farewell. Katherina, you may stay,
      For I have more to commune with Bianca.   *Exit.*
      Kate. Why, and I trust I may go too, may I not? What,
      shall I be appointed hours, as though, belike, I knew not
      what to take and what to leave? Ha!   *Exit.*
105 *Gremio.* You may go to the devil's dam. Your gifts are so
      good, here's none will hold you. Their love is not so
      great, Hortensio, but we may blow our nails together and
      fast it fairly out. Our cake's dough on both sides. Fare-
      well – yet for the love I bear my sweet Bianca, if I can
110 by any means light on a fit man to teach her that wherein
      she delights, I will wish him to her father.

85 *strange* unnatural 87 *mew* coop (term for caging a falcon) 92 *for* since
97 *Prefer* recommend *cunning* well-trained 101 *commune* discuss 103
belike presumably 105 *dam* mother 106 *hold* endure *Their* i.e. of
women 107 *blow . . . together* i.e. be patient 108 *Our cake's dough* i.e.
our expectations are disappointed (proverbial) 111 *wish* recommend

Hortensio. So will I, Signor Gremio. But a word, I pray.
Though the nature of our quarrel yet never brooked
parle, know now, upon advice, it toucheth us both — that
we may yet again have access to our fair mistress and be   115
happy rivals in Bianca's love — to labor and effect one
thing specially.

Gremio. What's that, I pray?

Hortensio. Marry, sir, to get a husband for her sister.

Gremio. A husband? A devil.   120

Hortensio. I say, a husband.

Gremio. I say, a devil. Think'st thou, Hortensio, though her
father be very rich, any man is so very a fool to be married to hell?

Hortensio. Tush, Gremio, though it pass your patience and   125
mine to endure her loud alarums, why, man, there be
good fellows in the world, an a man could light on them,
would take her with all her faults, and money enough.

Gremio. I cannot tell, but I had as lief take her dowry with
this condition, to be whipped at the high-cross every   130
morning.

Hortensio. Faith, as you say, there's small choice in rotten
apples. But come, since this bar in law makes us friends,
it shall be so far forth friendly maintained, till by helping
Baptista's eldest daughter to a husband we set his young-   135
est free for a husband, and then have to't afresh. Sweet
Bianca! Happy man be his dole. He that runs fastest gets
the ring. How say you, Signior Gremio?

Gremio. I am agreed, and would I had given him the best

113–14 *brooked parle* permitted discussion   114 *advice* reflection   123 *so
very a* such a complete   126 *alarums* calls to arms   127 *an* if   130 *high-
cross* market-cross   133 *bar* obstacle   136 *have to't* let us set to it   137
Happy . . . dole happiness be his lot (i.e. his who wins her; proverbial)
138 *ring* prize (playing on 'wedding-ring')

140   horse in Padua to begin his wooing that would thor-
        oughly woo her, wed her, and bed her, and rid the house
        of her. Come on.

                    Exeunt ambo. Manent Tranio and Lucentio.

        Tranio. I pray, sir, tell me, is it possible
            That love should of a sudden take such hold?
145   *Lucentio.* O Tranio, till I found it to be true
            I never thought it possible or likely.
            But see, while idly I stood looking on,
            I found the effect of love-in-idleness
            And now in plainness do confess to thee,
150   That art to me as secret and as dear
            As Anna to the Queen of Carthage was,
            Tranio, I burn, I pine, I perish, Tranio,
            If I achieve not this young modest girl.
            Counsel me, Tranio, for I know thou canst.
155   Assist me, Tranio, for I know thou wilt.
        Tranio. Master, it is no time to chide you now.
            Affection is not rated from the heart.
            If love have touched you, nought remains but so,
            'Redime te captum, quam queas minimo.'
160   *Lucentio.* Gramercies, lad. Go forward, this contents;
            The rest will comfort, for thy counsel's sound.
        Tranio. Master, you looked so longly on the maid,
            Perhaps you marked not what's the pith of all.
        Lucentio. O yes, I saw sweet beauty in her face,
165   Such as the daughter of Agenor had,

142 s.d. *ambo* both (Gremio and Hortensio)   *Manent* remain   148 *love-in-idleness* the pansy (supposed to have magical power in love)   151 *Anna* Dido's sister and confidante   153 *achieve* win   157 *rated* driven out by scolding   159 *Redime . . . minimo* redeem yourself from captivity as cheaply as you can (from the *Eunuchus* of Terence but quoted from Lilly's *Latin Grammar*)   162 *longly* longingly   165 *daughter of Agenor* Europa (loved by Jupiter, who abducted her in the shape of a bull)

That made great Jove to humble him to her hand
When with his knees he kissed the Cretan strand.
Tranio. Saw you no more? Marked you not how her sister
  Began to scold and raise up such a storm
  That mortal ears might hardly endure the din?   170
Lucentio. Tranio, I saw her coral lips to move,
  And with her breath she did perfume the air.
  Sacred and sweet was all I saw in her.
Tranio. Nay, then, 'tis time to stir him from his trance.
  I pray, awake, sir. If you love the maid   175
  Bend thoughts and wits to achieve her. Thus it stands:
  Her elder sister is so curst and shrewd
  That till the father rid his hands of her,
  Master, your love must live a maid at home,
  And therefore has he closely mewed her up,   180
  Because she will not be annoyed with suitors.
Lucentio. Ah, Tranio, what a cruel father's he.
  But art thou not advised he took some care
  To get her cunning schoolmasters to instruct her?
Tranio. Ay, marry, am I, sir, and now 'tis plotted.   185
Lucentio. I have it, Tranio.
Tranio.   Master, for my hand,
  Both our inventions meet and jump in one.
Lucentio. Tell me thine first.
Tranio.   You will be schoolmaster
  And undertake the teaching of the maid.
  That's your device.
Lucentio.   It is. May it be done?   190
Tranio. Not possible, for who shall bear your part

171–72 coral, perfume (hackneyed comparisons of the Petrarchan sonnet
tradition; cf. Shakespeare's Sonnet 130)   177 curst bad-tempered   shrewd
shrewish   180 mewed cooped   181 Because so that   183 advised aware
185 'tis plotted I have a plan   186 for I'll wager   187 inventions plans
jump agree

And be in Padua here Vincentio's son,
Keep house and ply his book, welcome his friends,
Visit his countrymen and banquet them?
195 *Lucentio.* Basta, content thee, for I have it full.
We have not yet been seen in any house
Nor can we be distinguished by our faces
For man or master. Then it follows thus.
Thou shalt be master, Tranio, in my stead,
200 Keep house and port and servants as I should.
I will some other be, some Florentine,
Some Neapolitan or meaner man of Pisa.
'Tis hatched and shall be so. Tranio, at once
Uncase thee, take my colored hat and cloak.
205 When Biondello comes he waits on thee,
But I will charm him first to keep his tongue.
Tranio. So had you need. *[They exchange cloaks and hats.]*
In brief, sir, sith it your pleasure is
And I am tied to be obedient —
210 For so your father charged me at our parting,
'Be serviceable to my son,' quoth he,
Although I think 'twas in another sense —
I am content to be Lucentio
Because so well I love Lucentio.
215 *Lucentio.* Tranio, be so, because Lucentio loves,
And let me be a slave, t'achieve that maid
Whose sudden sight hath thralled my wounded eye.

Enter Biondello.

Here comes the rogue. — Sirrah, where have you been?

195 *Basta* enough *have it full* see it clearly 200 *port* style of living
202 *meaner* i.e. of lower than my true rank 204 *Uncase* uncloak 208
sith since 217 *thralled* enslaved 218 *Sirrah* (usual form of address to an
inferior)

Biondello. Where have I been? Nay, how now, where are
   you?
   Master, has my fellow Tranio stol'n your clothes,   220
   Or you stol'n his, or both? Pray, what's the news?
Lucentio. Sirrah, come hither. 'Tis no time to jest,
   And therefore frame your manners to the time.
   Your fellow Tranio, here, to save my life,
   Puts my apparel and my count'nance on,   225
   And I for my escape have put on his,
   For in a quarrel since I came ashore
   I killed a man and fear I was descried.
   Wait you on him, I charge you, as becomes,
   While I make way from hence to save my life.   230
   You understand me?
Biondello.   I, sir? Ne'er a whit.
Lucentio. And not a jot of Tranio in your mouth.
   Tranio is changed into Lucentio.
Biondello. The better for him, would I were so too.
Tranio. So could I, faith, boy, to have the next wish
   after,   235
   That Lucentio indeed had Baptista's youngest daughter.
   But, sirrah, not for my sake but your master's, I advise
   You use your manners discreetly in all kind of companies.
   When I am alone, why then I am Tranio,
   But in all places else, your master Lucentio.   240
Lucentio. Tranio, let's go.
   One thing more rests, that thyself execute —
   To make one among these wooers. If thou ask me
   why,
   Sufficeth my reasons are both good and weighty.

                                       Exeunt.

225 *count'nance* appearance, deportment   242 *rests* remains *execute* ar-
range

The Presenters above speak.

245 *1. Servingman.* My lord, you nod, you do not mind the
     play.
     Sly. Yes, by Saint Anne, do I. A good matter, surely.
     Comes there any more of it?
     Page. My lord, 'tis but begun.
250 *Sly.* 'Tis a very excellent piece of work, madam lady —
     would 'twere done.

They sit and mark.

I, ii   *Enter [below] Petruchio and his man Grumio.*

Petruchio. Verona, for awhile I take my leave
          To see my friends in Padua, but of all
          My best belovèd and approvèd friend
          Hortensio; and I trow this is his house.
5   Here, sirrah Grumio, knock, I say.
Grumio. Knock, sir? Whom should I knock? Is there any
          man has rebused your worship?
Petruchio. Villain, I say, knock me here soundly.
Grumio. Knock you here, sir? Why, sir, what am I, sir,
10   that I should knock you here, sir?
Petruchio. Villain, I say, knock me at this gate,
          And rap me well or I'll knock your knave's pate.
Grumio. My master is grown quarrelsome. I should knock
          you first,
          And then I know after who comes by the worst.

244 S.D. *Presenters* choral characters of an induction who *present* the play
proper 245 *mind* pay attention to 251 S.D. *They sit and mark* (shortly
hereafter the presenters drop unnoticed out of the action) *mark* watch
I, ii S.D. *Petruchio* (diminutive of 'Pietro'; the *ch* is soft, not *Petrukio*)
Grumio (name from the *Mostellaria* of Plautus connoting 'clodhopper')
4 *trow* believe 7 *rebused* (Grumio's mistake for 'abused') 8 *me* i.e. for
me (but Grumio misunderstands, perhaps deliberately) 11 *gate* door

Petruchio. Will it not be?   15
   Faith, sirrah, an you'll not knock, I'll ring it.
   I'll try how you can sol, fa, and sing it.

                              He wrings him by the ears.
Grumio. Help, masters, help! My master is mad.
Petruchio. Now, knock when I bid you, sirrah villain.

                    Enter Hortensio.

Hortensio. How now, what's the matter? My old friend 20
   Grumio, and my good friend Petruchio! How do you all
   at Verona?
Petruchio. Signior Hortensio, come you to part
      the fray?
   Con tutto il cuore ben trovato, may I say.
Hortensio. Alla nostra casa ben venuto,   25
   Molto honorato signor mio Petruchio.
   Rise, Grumio, rise, we will compound this quarrel.
Grumio. Nay, 'tis no matter, sir, what he 'leges in Latin.
   If this be not a lawful cause for me to leave his service,
   look you, sir; he bid me knock him and rap him soundly, 30
   sir. Well, was it fit for a servant to use his master so,
   being perhaps, for aught I see, two and thirty, a pip out?
   Whom would to God I had well knocked at first,
   Then had not Grumio come by the worst.
Petruchio. A senseless villain. Good Hortensio,   35

---

16 *ring* (playing on 'wring')   17 *sol, fa* (playing on 'sowl,' pull by the
ears, and 'fay,' cleanse, i.e. beat)   18 *masters* i.e. the audience (comically
considered as bystanders)   24 *Con . . . trovato* with all my heart well met
25–26 *Alla . . . Petruchio* welcome to our house, my much honored
Signior Petruchio   27 *compound* settle   28 *'leges* alleges   32 *two . . . out*
drunk (a slang expression derived from the card-game of one and thirty;
a *pip* is a suit marking)

I bade the rascal knock upon your gate
And could not get him for my heart to do it.

Grumio. Knock at the gate? O heavens! Spake you not
  these words plain, 'Sirrah, knock me here, rap me here,
40 knock me well, and knock me soundly'? And come you
  now with 'knocking at the gate'?

Petruchio. Sirrah, be gone, or talk not, I advise you.

Hortensio. Petruchio, patience, I am Grumio's pledge.
  Why, this' a heavy chance 'twixt him and you,
45 Your ancient, trusty, pleasant servant Grumio.
  And tell me now, sweet friend, what happy gale
  Blows you to Padua here from old Verona?

Petruchio. Such wind as scatters young men through the
    world
  To seek their fortunes farther than at home,
50 Where small experience grows. But in a few,
  Signior Hortensio, thus it stands with me.
  Antonio my father is deceased,
  And I have thrust myself into this maze,
  Haply to wive and thrive as best I may.
55 Crowns in my purse I have and goods at home,
  And so am come abroad to see the world.

Hortensio. Petruchio, shall I then come roundly to thee
  And wish thee to a shrewd ill-favored wife?
  Thou'ldst thank me but a little for my counsel.
60 And yet I'll promise thee she shall be rich,
  And very rich — but th'art too much my friend
  And I'll not wish thee to her.

Petruchio. Signior Hortensio, 'twixt such friends as we
  Few words suffice. And therefore if thou know

---

44 *this'* this is   *heavy chance* sad event   50 *in a few* i.e. words   54 *Haply*
by chance   57 *come roundly* speak plainly   58 *shrewd* shrewish

One rich enough to be Petruchio's wife —   65
As wealth is burden of my wooing dance —
Be she as foul as was Florentius' love,
As old as Sibyl, and as curst and shrewd
As Socrates' Xanthippe, or a worse,
She moves me not, or not removes, at least,   70
Affection's edge in me, were she as rough
As are the swelling Adriatic seas.
I come to wive it wealthily in Padua —
If wealthily, then happily in Padua.

Grumio. Nay, look you, sir, he tells you flatly what his 75
mind is. Why, give him gold enough and marry him to
a puppet or an aglet-baby or an old trot with ne'er a
tooth in her head, though she have as many diseases as
two and fifty horses. Why, nothing comes amiss, so
money comes withal.   80

Hortensio. Petruchio, since we are stepped thus far in,
I will continue that I broached in jest.
I can, Petruchio, help thee to a wife
With wealth enough, and young and beauteous,
Brought up as best becomes a gentlewoman.   85
Her only fault — and that is faults enough —
Is that she is intolerable curst,
And shrewd and froward, so beyond all measure,

---

66 *burden* bass or undersong   67 *foul* ugly   *Florentius* (a knight who
married an old hag in return for the answer to a riddle—'What do women
most desire?'—that would save his life; she then turned into a beautiful
maiden; cf. Gower's *Confessio amantis*, Bk. I, or Chaucer's Wife of Bath's
Tale)   68 *Sibyl* the Cumaean Sibyl (a prophetess to whom Apollo
granted as many years of life as she could hold grains of sand in her hand)
69 *Xanthippe* the philosopher's wife (reputedly a shrew)   77 *aglet-baby*
tiny doll-figure (*aglet* indicating either a spangle or the metal 'point' of a
lace)   *trot* hag   80 *withal* at the same time   82 *that* that which   88 *froward* refractory

That were my state far worser than it is
90   I would not wed her for a mine of gold.
    Petruchio. Hortensio, peace. Thou know'st not gold's effect.
    Tell me her father's name, and 'tis enough,
    For I will board her though she chide as loud
    As thunder when the clouds in autumn crack.
95 *Hortensio.* Her father is Baptista Minola,
    An affable and courteous gentleman.
    Her name is Katherina Minola,
    Renowned in Padua for her scolding tongue.
    Petruchio. I know her father though I know not her,
100   And he knew my deceasèd father well.
    I will not sleep, Hortensio, till I see her,
    And therefore let me be thus bold with you,
    To give you over at this first encounter
    Unless you will accompany me thither.
105 *Grumio.* I pray you, sir, let him go while the humor lasts.
    A my word, an she knew him as well as I do, she would
    think scolding would do little good upon him. She may
    perhaps call him half a score knaves or so — why, that's
    nothing, an he begin once, he'll rail in his rope-tricks.
110   I'll tell you what, sir, an she stand him but a little, he will
    throw a figure in her face and so disfigure her with it
    that she shall have no more eyes to see withal than a
    cat. You know him not, sir.
    Hortensio. Tarry, Petruchio, I must go with thee,
115   For in Baptista's keep my treasure is.
    He hath the jewel of my life in hold,
    His youngest daughter, beautiful Bianca,

93 *board* (as in attacking a ship)   103 *give you over* leave you   105 *humor*
whim   106 *A* on, by   109 *rope-tricks* (Grumio's mistake for 'rhetoric,'
i.e. abusive language, with a glance at hanging)   110 *stand* withstand
111 *figure* rhetorical figure (i.e. a telling expression)   115 *keep* most
strongly fortified part of a castle   116 *hold* confinement

And her withholds from me and other more,
Suitors to her and rivals in my love,
Supposing it a thing impossible,   120
For those defects I have before rehearsed,
That ever Katherina will be wooed.
Therefore this order hath Baptista ta'en,
That none shall have access unto Bianca
Till Katherine the curst have got a husband.   125
Grumio. Katherine the curst!
  A title for a maid of all titles the worst.
Hortensio. Now shall my friend Petruchio do me grace
  And offer me, disguised in sober robes,
  To old Baptista as a schoolmaster   130
  Well seen in music, to instruct Bianca,
  That so I may, by this device, at least
  Have leave and leisure to make love to her
  And unsuspected court her by herself.

  *Enter Gremio [with a paper] and Lucentio disguised [as a
    schoolmaster].*

Grumio. Here's no knavery! See, to beguile the old folks, 135
  how the young folks lay their heads together! Master,
  master, look about you. Who goes there, ha?
Hortensio. Peace, Grumio, it is the rival of my love.
  Petruchio, stand by awhile.
Grumio. A proper stripling, and an amorous!   140
                              [They stand aside.]
Gremio. O very well, I have perused the note.
  Hark you, sir, I'll have them very fairly bound,
  All books of love, see that at any hand,

123 *order* measure 128 *grace* a favor 131 *seen* versed 140 *proper* handsome (ironically, of Gremio) 141 *note* (a list of books for Bianca) 143
at any hand in any case

And see you read no other lectures to her.
145　You understand me. Over and beside
　　Signior Baptista's liberality,
　　I'll mend it with a largess. Take your paper too,
　　And let me have them very well perfumed,
　　For she is sweeter than perfume itself
150　To whom they go to. What will you read to her?
　Lucentio. Whate'er I read to her, I'll plead for you,
　　As for my patron, stand you so assured,
　　As firmly as yourself were still in place,
　　Yea and perhaps with more successful words
155　Than you — unless you were a scholar, sir.
　Gremio. O this learning, what a thing it is!
　Grumio. [aside] O this woodcock, what an ass it is!
　Petruchio. Peace, sirrah.
　Hortensio. Grumio, mum! [advancing] God save you,
　　Signior Gremio.
160　Gremio. And you are well met, Signior Hortensio.
　　Trow you whither I am going? To Baptista Minola.
　　I promised to inquire carefully
　　About a schoolmaster for the fair Bianca,
　　And by good fortune I have lighted well
165　On this young man — for learning and behavior
　　Fit for her turn, well read in poetry
　　And other books, good ones, I warrant ye.
　Hortensio. 'Tis well, and I have met a gentleman
　　Hath promised me to help me to another,
170　A fine musician to instruct our mistress.

---

144 *read* teach　*lectures* lessons　147 *mend* increase　*largess* gift of money
paper i.e. the note　148 *them* i.e. the books　153 *in place* present　157
woodcock (bird easily caught, hence proverbially stupid)　161 *Trow* know
166 *turn* need　170 *mistress* beloved

58

So shall I no whit be behind in duty
To fair Bianca, so beloved of me.
Gremio. Beloved of me, and that my deeds shall prove.
Grumio. [*aside*] And that his bags shall prove.
Hortensio. Gremio, 'tis now no time to vent our love.   175
Listen to me, and if you speak me fair
I'll tell you news indifferent good for either.
Here is a gentleman whom by chance I met,
Upon agreement from us to his liking,
Will undertake to woo curst Katherine,   180
Yea and to marry her if her dowry please.
Gremio. So said, so done, is well.
Hortensio, have you told him all her faults?
Petruchio. I know she is an irksome brawling scold.
If that be all, masters, I hear no harm.   185
Gremio. No, sayst me so, friend? What countryman?
Petruchio. Born in Verona, old Antonio's son.
My father dead, my fortune lives for me,
And I do hope good days and long to see.
Gremio. O sir, such a life, with such a wife, were strange.   190
But if you have a stomach, to't a God's name,
You shall have me assisting you in all.
But will you woo this wildcat?
Petruchio.   Will I live?
Grumio. [*aside*] Will he woo her? Ay, or I'll hang her.
Petruchio. Why came I hither but to that intent?   195
Think you a little din can daunt mine ears?
Have I not in my time heard lions roar?
Have I not heard the sea, puffed up with winds,

---

174 *bags* moneybags 175 *vent* utter 177 *indifferent* equally 179 *agreement* terms (they will pay his expenses of wooing, l. 212) 180 *Will undertake* i.e. who, upon agreement, will undertake 191 *stomach* appetite *a in* 193 *Will I live?* i.e. certainly

Rage like an angry boar chafèd with sweat?
200 Have I not heard great ordnance in the field
And heaven's artillery thunder in the skies?
Have I not in a pitchèd battle heard
Loud 'larums, neighing steeds, and trumpets' clang?
And do you tell me of a woman's tongue,
205 That gives not half so great a blow to hear
As will a chestnut in a farmer's fire?
Tush, tush, fear boys with bugs.
Grumio. [aside]   For he fears none.
Gremio. Hortensio, hark.
This gentleman is happily arrived,
210 My mind presumes, for his own good and ours.
Hortensio. I promised we would be contributors,
And bear his charge of wooing whatsoe'er.
Gremio. And so we will, provided that he win her.
Grumio. [aside] I would I were as sure of a good dinner.

Enter Tranio brave [as Lucentio], and Biondello.

215 Tranio. Gentlemen, God save you. If I may be bold,
Tell me, I beseech you, which is the readiest way
To the house of Signior Baptista Minola?
Biondello. He that has the two fair daughters, is't you
mean?
Tranio. Even he, Biondello.
220 Gremio. Hark you, sir; you mean not her to —
Tranio. Perhaps him and her, sir, what have you to do?
Petruchio. Not her that chides, sir, at any hand, I pray.
Tranio. I love no chiders, sir. — Biondello, let's away.

---

203 *'larums* calls to arms   207 *fear* frighten   *bugs* bogeymen   208 *hark*
listen   212 *charge* expenses   214 s.d. *brave* finely dressed   221 *what
. . . do* what business is it of yours

Lucentio. [*aside*] Well begun, Tranio.

Hortensio.   Sir, a word ere you go.
  Are you a suitor to the maid you talk of, yea or no? 225

Tranio. An if I be, sir, is it any offense?

Gremio. No, if without more words you will get you
    hence.

Tranio. Why, sir, I pray, are not the streets as free
  For me as for you?

Gremio.   But so is not she.

Tranio. For what reason, I beseech you?

Gremio.   For this reason, if you'll know, 230
  That she's the choice love of Signior Gremio.

Hortensio. That she's the chosen of Signior Hortensio.

Tranio. Softly, my masters. If you be gentlemen,
  Do me this right, hear me with patience.
  Baptista is a noble gentleman,   235
  To whom my father is not all unknown,
  And were his daughter fairer than she is
  She may more suitors have, and me for one.
  Fair Leda's daughter had a thousand wooers,
  Then well one more may fair Bianca have.   240
  And so she shall: Lucentio shall make one,
  Though Paris came in hope to speed alone.

Gremio. What, this gentleman will out-talk us all.

Lucentio. Sir, give him head. I know he'll prove a jade.

Petruchio. Hortensio, to what end are all these words?   245

Hortensio. Sir, let me be so bold as ask you,
  Did you yet ever see Baptista's daughter?

Tranio. No, sir, but hear I do that he hath two,

---

239 *Leda's daughter* Helen of Troy (Leda was made love to by Jupiter in
the shape of a swan) 240 *one more* i.e. than she now has 242 *Paris*
Helen's lover (who took her away from her husband Menelaus) *came*
were to come *speed* succeed 244 *jade* worthless horse (easily tired)

The one as famous for a scolding tongue
250 As is the other for beauteous modesty.
Petruchio. Sir, sir, the first's for me, let her go by.
Gremio. Yea, leave that labor to great Hercules,
    And let it be more than Alcides' twelve.
Petruchio. Sir, understand you this of me, in sooth.
255 The youngest daughter, whom you hearken for,
    Her father keeps from all access of suitors
    And will not promise her to any man
    Until the elder sister first be wed.
    The younger then is free, and not before.
260 *Tranio.* If it be so, sir, that you are the man
    Must stead us all, and me amongst the rest,
    And if you break the ice and do this feat,
    Achieve the elder, set the younger free
    For our access, whose hap shall be to have her
265 Will not so graceless be to be ingrate.
Hortensio. Sir, you say well, and well you do conceive,
    And since you do profess to be a suitor,
    You must, as we do, gratify this gentleman,
    To whom we all rest generally beholding.
270 *Tranio.* Sir, I shall not be slack, in sign whereof,
    Please ye we may contrive this afternoon
    And quaff carouses to our mistress' health,
    And do as adversaries do in law,
    Strive mightily but eat and drink as friends.
Grumio, Biondello. O excellent motion! Fellows, let's be
275   gone.

253 *Alcides* Hercules (grandson of Alcaeus) 254 *sooth* truth 255 *hearken*
lie in wait 261 *stead* help 263 *Achieve* win 264 *whose hap* he whose
luck 266 *well you do conceive* you have hit on a good idea 268 *gratify*
recompense 271 *contrive* while away 273 *adversaries* i.e. lawyers (not
their clients)

Hortensio. The motion's good indeed, and be it so.
  Petruchio, I shall be your ben venuto.   *Exeunt.*

Enter Kate and Bianca [with her hands tied].   II, i

Bianca. Good sister, wrong me not, nor wrong yourself,
  To make a bondmaid and a slave of me —
  That I disdain. But for these other gawds,
  Unbind my hands, I'll pull them off myself,
  Yea, all my raiment, to my petticoat,   5
  Or what you will command me will I do,
  So well I know my duty to my elders.
Kate. Of all thy suitors, here I charge thee, tell
  Whom thou lov'st best. See thou dissemble not.
Bianca. Believe me, sister, of all the men alive   10
  I never yet beheld that special face
  Which I could fancy more than any other.
Kate. Minion, thou liest. Is't not Hortensio?
Bianca. If you affect him, sister, here I swear
  I'll plead for you myself but you shall have him.   15
Kate. O then, belike, you fancy riches more.
  You will have Gremio to keep you fair.
Bianca. Is it for him you do envy me so?
  Nay, then you jest, and now I well perceive
  You have but jested with me all this while.   20
  I prithee, sister Kate, untie my hands.
Kate. If that be jest then all the rest was so.   *Strikes her.*

277 *ben venuto* welcome   II, i, 3 *gawds* ornaments   13 *Minion* minx   14
affect love   16 *belike* probably   17 *fair* in finery   18 *envy* hate

Enter Baptista.

Baptista. Why, how now, dame, whence grows this in-
    solence?

Bianca, stand aside. Poor girl, she weeps.

25   Go ply thy needle, meddle not with her.

For shame, thou hilding of a devilish spirit,

Why dost thou wrong her that did ne'er wrong thee?

When did she cross thee with a bitter word?

Kate. Her silence flouts me and I'll be revenged.

                                        Flies after Bianca.

30 *Baptista.* What, in my sight? Bianca, get thee in.

                                        Exit [Bianca].

Kate. What, will you not suffer me? Nay, now I see

She is your treasure, she must have a husband;

I must dance barefoot on her wedding-day,

And for your love to her lead apes in hell.

35   Talk not to me, I will go sit and weep

Till I can find occasion of revenge.   *[Exit.]*

Baptista. Was ever gentleman thus grieved as I?

But who comes here?

*Enter Gremio [with] Lucentio [as a schoolmaster] in
the habit of a mean man, Petruchio with [Hortensio
as a music-master, and] Tranio [as Lucentio] with
his boy [Biondello] bearing a lute and books.*

Gremio. Good morrow, neighbor Baptista.

40 *Baptista.* Good morrow, neighbor Gremio. God save you,
    gentlemen.

Petruchio. And you, good sir. Pray, have you not a daugh-
    ter

26 *hilding* good-for-nothing   33 *dance . . . day* (customary for an elder
unmarried sister)   34 *lead . . . hell* (proverbial fate of old maids)   38 S.D.
mean of low social station   *boy* page

Called Katherina, fair and virtuous?
Baptista. I have a daughter, sir, called Katherina.
Gremio. You are too blunt, go to it orderly.   45
Petruchio. You wrong me, Signior Gremio, give me leave.
  I am a gentlemen of Verona, sir,
  That, hearing of her beauty and her wit,
  Her affability and bashful modesty,
  Her wondrous qualities and mild behavior,   50
  Am bold to show myself a forward guest
  Within your house, to make mine eye the witness
  Of that report which I so oft have heard.
  And for an entrance to my entertainment
  I do present you with a man of mine,   55

                           [presenting Hortensio]
  Cunning in music and the mathematics,
  To instruct her fully in those sciences,
  Whereof I know she is not ignorant.
  Accept of him or else you do me wrong.
  His name is Litio, born in Mantua.   60
Baptista. Y'are welcome, sir, and he for your good sake.
  But for my daughter Katherine, this I know,
  She is not for your turn, the more my grief.
Petruchio. I see you do not mean to part with her,
  Or else you like not of my company.   65
Baptista. Mistake me not, I speak but as I find.
  Whence are you, sir? What may I call your name?
Petruchio. Petruchio is my name, Antonio's son,
  A man well known throughout all Italy.
Baptista. I know him well, you are welcome for his sake.   70

---

54 **entrance** entrance fee *entertainment* welcome (as a suitor) 60 *Litio*
(or *Lizio*, an old Italian word for garlic; pronounced *Leét-sio*) 63 *turn*
purpose 70 *know him* i.e. know who he is

Gremio. Saving your tale, Petruchio, I pray, let us, that are
poor petitioners, speak too. Backare, you are marvellous
forward.

Petruchio. O pardon me, Signior Gremio, I would fain be
doing.

75 *Gremio.* I doubt it not, sir, but you will curse your wooing.
Neighbor, this is a gift very grateful, I am sure of it. To
express the like kindness, myself, that have been more
kindly beholding to you than any, freely give unto you
this young scholar, *[presenting Lucentio]* that hath been
80 long studying at Rheims; as cunning in Greek, Latin,
and other languages as the other in music and mathematics. His name is Cambio, pray accept his service.

Baptista. A thousand thanks, Signior Gremio. Welcome,
good Cambio. *[to Tranio]* But, gentle sir, methinks you
85 walk like a stranger. May I be so bold to know the cause
of your coming?

Tranio. Pardon me, sir, the boldness is mine own,
That, being a stranger in this city here,
Do make myself a suitor to your daughter,
90 Unto Bianca, fair and virtuous.
Nor is your firm resolve unknown to me
In the preferment of the eldest sister.
This liberty is all that I request,
That, upon knowledge of my parentage,
95 I may have welcome 'mongst the rest that woo,
And free access and favor as the rest.
And toward the education of your daughters
I here bestow a simple instrument,

---

71 *Saving* with no disrespect to   72 *Backare* stand back   (mock Latin)
74 *fain* gladly   80 *Rheims* (here pronounced *reams*)   82 *Cambio* (the
word means 'exchange' in Italian)   88 *That* I who

And this small packet of Greek and Latin books.
If you accept them, then their worth is great.   100
Baptista. Lucentio is your name, of whence, I pray?
Tranio. Of Pisa, sir, son to Vincentio.
Baptista. A mighty man of Pisa by report,
   I know him well. You are very welcome, sir.
   [To Hortensio] Take you that lute, *[to Lucentio]* and
      you the set of books.   105
   You shall go see your pupils presently.
   Holla, within!

Enter a Servant.

Sirrah, lead these gentlemen
To my daughters, and tell them both
These are their tutors; bid them use them well.   110
                    *[Exit Servant with Hortensio,
                        Lucentio, and Biondello.]*
   We will go walk a little in the orchard
   And then to dinner. You are passing welcome,
   And so I pray you all to think yourselves.
Petruchio. Signior Baptista, my business asketh haste,
   And every day I cannot come to woo.   115
   You knew my father well, and in him me,
   Left solely heir to all his lands and goods,
   Which I have bettered rather than decreased.
   Then tell me, if I get your daughter's love
   What dowry shall I have with her to wife?   120
Baptista. After my death the one half of my lands,
   And in possession twenty thousand crowns.
Petruchio. And for that dowry, I'll assure her of

104 *know him* i.e. know who he is 106 *presently* immediately 111
orchard garden 112 *passing* surpassingly 122 *possession* i.e. immediate
possession

Her widowhood, be it that she survive me,
125 In all my lands and leases whatsoever.
Let specialties be therefore drawn between us,
That covenants may be kept on either hand.
Baptista. Ay, when the special thing is well obtained,
That is, her love, for that is all in all.
130 *Petruchio.* Why, that is nothing, for I tell you, father,
I am as peremptory as she proud-minded,
And where two raging fires meet together
They do consume the thing that feeds their fury.
Though little fire grows great with little wind,
135 Yet extreme gusts will blow out fire and all.
So I to her, and so she yields to me,
For I am rough and woo not like a babe.
Baptista. Well mayst thou woo, and happy be thy speed,
But be thou armed for some unhappy words.
140 *Petruchio.* Ay, to the proof, as mountains are for winds,
That shakes not though they blow perpetually.

Enter Hortensio [as Litio] with his head broke.

Baptista. How now, my friend, why dost thou look so pale?
Hortensio. For fear, I promise you, if I look pale.
Baptista. What, will my daughter prove a good musician?
145 *Hortensio.* I think she'll sooner prove a soldier.
Iron may hold with her but never lutes.
Baptista. Why, then thou canst not break her to the lute?
Hortensio. Why, no, for she hath broke the lute to me.
I did but tell her she mistook her frets

124 *widowhood* income if widowed   126 *specialties* contracts   131 *peremptory* determined   138 *speed* fortune   140 *to the proof* in tested armor
141 S.D. *broke* i.e. with the skin broken, bleeding   146 *lutes* (playing on
'cement made of clay')   147 *break* tame   149 *frets* rings of gut placed
on the fingerboard to regulate the fingering (Kate quibbled on *fret and
fume*, be indignant)

And bowed her hand to teach her fingering,   150
When, with a most impatient devilish spirit,
'Frets, call you these?' quoth she, 'I'll fume with them.'
And with that word she struck me on the head,
And through the instrument my pate made way,
And there I stood amazèd for a while   155
As on a pillory, looking through the lute,
While she did call me rascal, fiddler,
And twangling Jack, with twenty such vile terms,
As had she studied to misuse me so.
Petruchio. Now, by the world, it is a lusty wench.   160
I love her ten times more than e'er I did.
O how I long to have some chat with her!
Baptista. *[to Hortensio]* Well, go with me, and be not so
    discomfited.
Proceed in practice with my younger daughter.
She's apt to learn and thankful for good turns.   165
Signior Petruchio, will you go with us
Or shall I send my daughter Kate to you?
Petruchio. I pray you do. I will attend her here,
        Exit [Baptista with Gremio, Tranio, and
            Hortensio]. Manet Petruchio.
And woo her with some spirit when she comes.
Say that she rail, why then I'll tell her plain   170
She sings as sweetly as a nightingale.
Say that she frown, I'll say she looks as clear
As morning roses newly washed with dew.
Say she be mute and will not speak a word,
Then I'll commend her volubility   175
And say she uttereth piercing eloquence.
If she do bid me pack I'll give her thanks

150 *bowed* bent 158 *Jack* knave 160 *lusty* lively 165 *apt* willing
168 *attend* wait for

As though she bid me stay by her a week.
If she deny to wed I'll crave the day
180 When I shall ask the banns, and when be marrièd.

Enter Kate.

But here she comes, and now, Petruchio, speak.
Good morrow, Kate, for that's your name, I hear.
Kate. Well have you heard, but something hard of hearing.
They call me Katherine that do talk of me.
185 *Petruchio.* You lie, in faith, for you are called plain Kate,
And bonny Kate, and sometimes Kate the curst.
But Kate, the prettiest Kate in Christendom,
Kate of Kate-Hall, my super-dainty Kate,
For dainties are all cates, and therefore, Kate,
190 Take this of me, Kate of my consolation:
Hearing thy mildness praised in every town,
Thy virtues spoke of, and thy beauty sounded,
Yet not so deeply as to thee belongs,
Myself am moved to woo thee for my wife.
Kate. Moved? In good time: let him that moved you
195   hither
Remove you hence. I knew you at the first,
You were a movable.
Petruchio. Why, what's a movable?
Kate. A joint-stool.
200 *Petruchio.* Thou hast hit it: come sit on me.
Kate. Asses are made to bear, and so are you.

179 *deny* refuse   180 *ask the banns* announce in church the intent to marry
183 *hard* (playing on *heard,* pronounced similarly)   186 *bonny* strapping
189 *dainties* delicacies   *cates* choice foods (playing, of course, on *Kates*)
192 *sounded* proclaimed (with a play, in *deeply,* on 'plumbed')   195 *In good
time* indeed   197 *movable* (quibbling on 'piece of furniture')   199 *joint-
stool* stool made by a joiner   201 *bear* i.e. carry (Petruchio quibbles on
'bear children')

Petruchio. Women are made to bear, and so are you.

Kate. No such jade as you, if me you mean.

Petruchio. Alas, good Kate, I will not burden thee,
   For knowing thee to be but young and light.   205

Kate. Too light for such a swain as you to catch,
   And yet as heavy as my weight should be.

Petruchio. Should be? should – buzz!

Kate.   Well ta'en, and like a buzzard.

Petruchio. O slow-winged turtle! Shall a buzzard take
   thee?

Kate. Ay, for a turtle, as he takes a buzzard.   210

Petruchio. Come, come, you wasp, i' faith you are too
   angry.

Kate. If I be waspish best beware my sting.

Petruchio. My remedy is then to pluck it out.

Kate. Ay, if the fool could find it where it lies.

Petruchio. Who knows not where a wasp does wear his
   sting?   215
  In his tail.

Kate. In his tongue.

Petruchio. Whose tongue?

Kate. Yours, if you talk of tales, and so farewell.

Petruchio. What, with my tongue in your tail?   220
  Nay, come again, good Kate, I am a gentleman.

Kate. That I'll try.   *She strikes him.*

Petruchio. I swear I'll cuff you if you strike again.

Kate. So may you lose your arms.

203 *jade* worthless horse (playing on *Asses* and quibbling on *bear* in the
sense of 'support a male in the sexual act')   205 *For knowing* because I
know   *light* (playing on a 'light' song, i.e. one without a *burden*, or bass
undersong)   206 *swain* rustic lover   208 *buzz* (an expression of con-
tempt, playing on *be*)   *buzzard* fool (Petruchio quibbles on 'an inferior
kind of hawk, useless for falconry')   209 *turtle* turtledove   210 *buzzard*
buzzing insect (suggesting *wasp*)   224 *arms* coat of arms

225 If you strike me you are no gentleman,
        And if no gentleman, why then no arms.
     Petruchio. A herald, Kate? O put me in thy books.
     Kate. What is your crest, a coxcomb?
     Petruchio. A combless cock, so Kate will be my hen.
230 *Kate.* No cock of mine, you crow too like a craven.
     Petruchio. Nay, come, Kate, come, you must not look so
        sour.
     Kate. It is my fashion when I see a crab.
     Petruchio. Why, here's no crab, and therefore look not
        sour.
     Kate. There is, there is.
     Petruchio. Then show it me.
235 *Kate.*   Had I a glass I would.
     Petruchio. What, you mean my face?
     Kate. Well aimed of such a young one.
     Petruchio. Now, by Saint George, I am too young for you.
     Kate. Yet you are withered.
240 *Petruchio.* 'Tis with cares.
     Kate. I care not.
     Petruchio. Nay, hear you, Kate, in sooth you 'scape not so.
     Kate. I chafe you if I tarry; let me go.
     Petruchio. No, not a whit. I find you passing gentle.
245 'Twas told me you were rough and coy and sullen,
        And now I find report a very liar,
        For thou art pleasant, gamesome, passing courteous,
        But slow in speech, yet sweet as springtime flowers.
        Thou canst not frown, thou canst not look askance,

227 *in thy books* in your heraldic registers (playing on 'in your good graces') 228 *crest* armorial device *coxcomb* cap of a court fool (playing on *crest*, comb; Petruchio then quibbles on 'cock's comb') 229 *combless* gentle (with *comb* or crest cut down) 230 *craven* cock that will not fight 232 *crab* crab-apple 235 *glass* looking-glass 237 *aimed of* guessed for *young* inexperienced 242 *sooth* truth 245 *coy* haughty 249 *askance* scornfully

Nor bite the lip as angry wenches will,   250
Nor hast thou pleasure to be cross in talk.
But thou with mildness entertain'st thy wooers,
With gentle conference, soft and affable.
Why does the world report that Kate doth limp?
O sland'rous world! Kate like the hazel-twig   255
Is straight and slender, and as brown in hue
As hazelnuts and sweeter than the kernels.
O let me see thee walk. Thou dost not halt.
Kate. Go, fool, and whom thou keep'st command.
Petruchio. Did ever Dian so become a grove   260
   As Kate this chamber with her princely gait?
   O be thou Dian and let her be Kate,
   And then let Kate be chaste and Dian sportful.
Kate. Where did you study all this goodly speech?
Petruchio. It is extempore, from my mother-wit.   265
Kate. A witty mother, witless else her son.
Petruchio. Am I not wise?
Kate. Yes, keep you warm.
Petruchio. Marry, so I mean, sweet Katherine, in thy bed.
   And therefore, setting all this chat aside,   270
   Thus in plain terms. Your father hath consented
   That you shall be my wife, your dowry 'greed on,
   And will you, nill you, I will marry you.
   Now, Kate, I am a husband for your turn,
   For by this light, whereby I see thy beauty —   275
   Thy beauty that doth make me like thee well —
   Thou must be married to no man but me,

---

258 *halt* limp   259 *whom thou keep'st* i.e. your servants   260 *Dian* Diana
(goddess of virginity and of the hunt)   263 *sportful* amorous   265 *mother-
wit* native intelligence 266 *witless . . . son* otherwise her son would be witless (his only wit being inherited from her)   268 *keep you warm* i.e. take
care of yourself (to have the wit or wisdom to keep warm being proverbial)   273 *nill you* will you not   274 *for your turn* to suit you

Enter Baptista, Gremio, [and] Tranio [as Lucentio].

For I am he am born to tame you, Kate,
And bring you from a wild Kate to a Kate
280   Conformable as other household Kates.
Here comes your father. Never make denial,
I must and will have Katherine to my wife.
Baptista. Now, Signior Petruchio, how speed you with my
daughter?
Petruchio. How but well, sir? How but well?
285   It were impossible I should speed amiss.
Baptista. Why, how now, daughter Katherine? In your
dumps?
Kate. Call you me daughter? Now, I promise you
You have showed a tender fatherly regard
To wish me wed to one half lunatic,
290   A madcap ruffian and a swearing Jack,
That thinks with oaths to face the matter out.
Petruchio. Father, 'tis thus. Yourself and all the world
That talked of her have talked amiss of her.
If she be curst it is for policy,
295   For she's not froward but modest as the dove.
She is not hot but temperate as the morn.
For patience she will prove a second Grissel,
And Roman Lucrece for her chastity.
And, to conclude, we have 'greed so well together
300   That upon Sunday is the wedding-day.
Kate. I'll see thee hanged on Sunday first.

279 *wild Kate* (punning on 'wild cat') 283 *speed* succeed 287 *promise*
assure 291 *face* brazen 294 *policy* cunning 296 *hot* of angry disposition
297 *Grissel* Griselda (the epitome of wifely patience and obedience; cf.
Boccaccio's *Decameron*, X, 10, or Chaucer's Clerk's Tale) 298 *Lucrece*
(she killed herself after being raped by Sextus Tarquinius, hence became
the epitome of wifely chastity and honor; cf. Shakespeare's *Rape of Lucrece*)

Gremio. Hark, Petruchio, she says she'll see thee hanged
  first.

Tranio. Is this your speeding? Nay, then good night our
  part!

Petruchio. Be patient, gentlemen, I choose her for myself.
  If she and I be pleased, what's that to you?   305
  'Tis bargained 'twixt us twain, being alone,
  That she shall still be curst in company.
  I tell you, 'tis incredible to believe
  How much she loves me. O the kindest Kate!
  She hung about my neck, and kiss on kiss   310
  She vied so fast, protesting oath on oath,
  That in a twink she won me to her love.
  O you are novices. 'Tis a world to see
  How tame, when men and women are alone,
  A meacock wretch can make the curstest shrew.   315
  Give me thy hand, Kate, I will unto Venice
  To buy apparel 'gainst the wedding-day.
  Provide the feast, father, and bid the guests.
  I will be sure my Katherine shall be fine.

Baptista. I know not what to say — but give me your hands.   320
  God send you joy! Petruchio, 'tis a match.

Gremio, Tranio. Amen, say we, we will be witnesses.

Petruchio. Father, and wife, and gentlemen, adieu.
  I will to Venice. Sunday comes apace.
  We will have rings and things and fine array,   325
  And kiss me, Kate, [*sings*] 'We will be married a Sunday.'
                       Exeunt Petruchio and Kate [severally].

Gremio. Was ever match clapped up so suddenly?

303 *speeding* success 311 *vied* i.e. went me one better (cardplaying term)
313 *world* i.e. worth a world 315 *meacock* cowardly 317 *'gainst* in anticipation of 319 *fine* finely dressed 326 s.d. *severally* at different doors
327 *match* contract (with a play on 'mating') *clapped up* shaken hands
on, agreed to

Baptista. Faith, gentlemen, now I play a merchant's part
    And venture madly on a desperate mart.
330 *Tranio.* 'Twas a commodity lay fretting by you.
    'Twill bring you gain or perish on the seas.
Baptista. The gain I seek is quiet in the match.
Gremio. No doubt but he hath got a quiet catch.
    But now, Baptista, to your younger daughter.
335   Now is the day we long have lookèd for.
    I am your neighbor and was suitor first.
Tranio. And I am one that love Bianca more
    Than words can witness or your thoughts can guess.
Gremio. Youngling, thou canst not love so dear as I.
Tranio. Greybeard, thy love doth freeze.
340 *Gremio.*   But thine doth fry.
    Skipper, stand back, 'tis age that nourisheth.
Tranio. But youth in ladies' eyes that flourisheth.
Baptista. Content you, gentlemen, I will compound this
    strife.
    'Tis deeds must win the prize, and he of both
345   That can assure my daughter greatest dower
    Shall have my Bianca's love.
    Say, Signior Gremio, what can you assure her?
Gremio. First, as you know, my house within the city
    Is richly furnishèd with plate and gold,
350   Basins and ewers to lave her dainty hands;
    My hangings all of Tyrian tapestry;
    In ivory coffers I have stuffed my crowns;
    In cypress chests my arras counterpoints,

---

329 *mart* bargain   330 *fretting* (of a stored commodity that decays, as wool
'fretted' by moths; with a play on 'chafing')   341 *Skipper* flighty youth
343 *compound* settle   344 *he of both* whichever of the two (of you)   345
assure guarantee   350 *lave* wash   351 *Tyrian* purple   353 *arras counter-
points* counterpanes of Arras tapestry

Costly apparel, tents, and canopies,
Fine linen, Turkey cushions bossed with pearl,   355
Valance of Venice gold in needlework,
Pewter and brass, and all things that belongs
To house or housekeeping. Then at my farm
I have a hundred milch-kine to the pail,
Six score fat oxen standing in my stalls,   360
And all things answerable to this portion.
Myself am struck in years, I must confess,
And if I die to-morrow this is hers,
If whilst I live she will be only mine.
Tranio. That 'only' came well in. Sir, list to me.   365
I am my father's heir and only son.
If I may have your daughter to my wife
I'll leave her houses three or four as good,
Within rich Pisa walls, as any one
Old Signior Gremio has in Padua,   370
Besides two thousand ducats by the year
Of fruitful land, all which shall be her jointure.
What, have I pinched you, Signior Gremio?
Gremio. Two thousand ducats by the year of land!
[*Aside*] My land amounts not to so much in all.   375
That she shall have, besides an argosy
That now is lying in Marseilles' road.
What, have I choked you with an argosy?
Tranio. Gremio, 'tis known my father hath no less
Than three great argosies, besides two galliasses   380

354 *tents* (meaning doubtful; perhaps hangings of some sort) *canopies*
testers 355 *bossed* embroidered 356 *Valance* drapery round the canopy
or frame of a bed 359 *milch-kine* cows *to the pail* i.e. in a dairy 362
struck advanced 371 *ducats* gold coins 372 *Of* from *jointure* settlement
376 *argosy* large merchant-ship 377 *Marseilles'* (here pronounced *Mar-
séllus*) *road* harbor 380 *galliasses* large galleys

And twelve tight galleys. These I will assure her
And twice as much whate'er thou off'rest next.

Gremio. Nay, I have off'red all, I have no more,
And she can have no more than all I have.

385 If you like me, she shall have me and mine.

Tranio. Why, then the maid is mine from all the world
By your firm promise. Gremio is outvied.

Baptista. I must confess your offer is the best,
And let your father make her the assurance,

390 She is your own, else you must pardon me.
If you should die before him, where's her dower?

Tranio. That's but a cavil. He is old, I young.

Gremio. And may not young men die as well as old?

Baptista. Well, gentlemen, I am thus resolved.

395 On Sunday next, you know,
My daughter Katherine is to be married.
Now on the Sunday following shall Bianca
Be bride to you, if you make this assurance.
If not, to Signior Gremio.

400 And so I take my leave and thank you both.   *Exit.*

Gremio. Adieu, good neighbor. Now I fear thee not.
Sirrah young gamester, your father were a fool
To give thee all and in his waning age
Set foot under thy table. Tut, a toy!

405 An old Italian fox is not so kind, my boy.   *Exit.*

Tranio. A vengeance on your crafty withered hide!
Yet I have faced it with a card of ten.
'Tis in my head to do my master good.
I see no reason but supposed Lucentio

---

381 *tight* i.e. well caulked   387 *outvied* outbid   389 *assurance* guarantee
402 *Sirrah* (contemptuous to a person of equal rank)   *were* would be   404
Set . . . table i.e. become your dependent   *a toy* nonsense   407 *faced . . .*
ten bluffed successfully with a ten-spot

Must get a father, called supposed Vincentio; 410
And that's a wonder. Fathers commonly
Do get their children, but in this case of wooing
A child shall get a sire if I fail not of my cunning.

Exit.

Enter Lucentio [as Cambio], Hortensio [as Litio], and III, i
Bianca.

Lucentio. Fiddler, forbear, you grow too forward, sir.
Have you so soon forgot the entertainment
Her sister Katherine welcomed you withal?
Hortensio. But, wrangling pedant, this is
The patroness of heavenly harmony. 5
Then give me leave to have prerogative,
And when in music we have spent an hour
Your lecture shall have leisure for as much.
Lucentio. Preposterous ass, that never read so far
To know the cause why music was ordained! 10
Was it not to refresh the mind of man
After his studies or his usual pain?
Then give me leave to read philosophy,
And while I pause, serve in your harmony.
Hortensio. Sirrah, I will not bear these braves of thine. 15
Bianca. Why, gentlemen, you do me double wrong
To strive for that which resteth in my choice.
I am no breeching scholar in the schools.

412 *get* beget   III, i, 5 *patroness* goddess (i.e. Minerva, goddess of music
and inventor of musical instruments; cf. I, i, 84)   6 *prerogative* precedence
8 *lecture* lesson   9 *Preposterous* reversing the natural order of things
12 *pain* toil   13 *read* teach   15 *braves* insults   18 *breeching scholar* school-
boy liable to whipping

I'll not be tied to hours nor 'pointed times,

20 But learn my lessons as I please myself.

And, to cut off all strife, here sit we down.

Take you your instrument, play you the whiles;

His lecture will be done ere you have tuned.

Hortensio. You'll leave his lecture when I am in tune?

25 *Lucentio.* That will be never. Tune your instrument.

Bianca. Where left we last?

Lucentio. Here, madam: [*Reads.*]

   'Hic ibat Simois, hic est Sigeia tellus,

    Hic steterat Priami regia celsa senis.'

30 *Bianca.* Conster them.

Lucentio. 'Hic ibat,' as I told you before; 'Simois,' I am

Lucentio; 'hic est,' son unto Vincentio of Pisa; 'Sigeia

tellus,' disguised thus to get your love; 'Hic steterat,' and

that Lucentio that comes a wooing; 'Priami,' is my man

35 Tranio; 'regia,' bearing my port; 'celsa senis,' that we

might beguile the old pantaloon.

Hortensio. Madam, my instrument's in tune.

Bianca. Let's hear. [*He plays.*] O fie, the treble jars.

Lucentio. Spit in the hole, man, and tune again.

40 *Bianca.* Now let me see if I can conster it.

'Hic ibat Simois,' I know you not; 'hic est Sigeia tellus,'

I trust you not; 'Hic steterat Priami,' take heed he hear us

not; 'regia,' presume not; 'celsa senis,' despair not.

Hortensio. Madam, 'tis now in tune.

---

21 *And . . . down* (apparently all three sit together on a bench) 22 *the whiles* meanwhile 28–29 *Hic . . . senis* here flowed the Simois, here lies the Sigeian plain, here stood the lofty palace of old Priam (Ovid, *Epistolae Heroidum*, I, a letter from Penelope to Ulysses) 30 *Conster* construe (translate) 35 *bearing my port* behaving as I would 36 *pantaloon* foolish old man (stock character of the *commedia dell' arte*) 38 *jars* is discordant 39 *Spit in the hole* (to make the peg hold)

Lucentio.   All but the bass.

Hortensio. The bass is right, 'tis the base knave that jars.   **45**
　　[Aside] How fiery and forward our pedant is!
　　Now, for my life, the knave doth court my love.
　　Pedascule, I'll watch you better yet.

Bianca. In time I may believe, yet I mistrust.

Lucentio. Mistrust it not, for sure Aeacides   **50**
　　Was Ajax, called so from his grandfather.

Bianca. I must believe my master, else I promise you,
　　I should be arguing still upon that doubt.
　　But let it rest. Now, Litio, to you.
　　Good master, take it not unkindly, pray,   **55**
　　That I have been thus pleasant with you both.

Hortensio. You may go walk and give me leave a while.
　　My lessons make no music in three parts.

Lucentio. Are you so formal, sir? *[aside]* Well, I must wait
　　And watch withal, for but I be deceived,   **60**
　　Our fine musician groweth amorous.

Hortensio. Madam, before you touch the instrument
　　To learn the order of my fingering,
　　I must begin with rudiments of art,
　　To teach you gamut in a briefer sort,   **65**
　　More pleasant, pithy, and effectual
　　Than hath been taught by any of my trade.
　　And there it is in writing, fairly drawn.

Bianca. Why, I am past my gamut long ago.

Hortensio. Yet read the gamut of Hortensio.   **70**

---

46 *pedant* schoolmaster or tutor   48 *Pedascule* (Latin coinage from *pedant*, contemptuously diminutive)   50 *Aeacides* descendant of Aeacus (Lucentio explains a reference in the line of Ovid's epistle which follows immediately after the two lines already quoted)   51 *Ajax* one of the Greek heroes at Troy   58 *in three parts* for three voices   59 *formal* precise   60 *withal* at the same time   *but* unless   65 *gamut* the scale

Bianca. *[reads]*

> 'Gamut I am, the ground of all accord,
> A re, to plead Hortensio's passion;
> B mi, Bianca, take him for thy lord,
> C fa ut, that loves with all affection;
> 75   D sol re, one clef, two notes have I;
> E la mi, show pity or I die.'

Call you this gamut? Tut, I like it not.
Old fashions please me best; I am not so nice
To change true rules for odd inventions.

Enter a Messenger.

80 *Messenger.* Mistress, your father prays you leave your books
    And help to dress your sister's chamber up.
    You know to-morrow is the wedding day.
Bianca. Farewell, sweet masters both, I must be gone.

                [Exeunt Bianca and Messenger.]

Lucentio. Faith, mistress, then I have no cause to stay.

                [Exit.]

85 *Hortensio.* But I have cause to pry into this pedant.
    Methinks he looks as though he were in love.
    Yet if thy thoughts, Bianca, be so humble
    To cast thy wand'ring eyes on every stale,
    Seize thee that list. If once I find thee ranging,
90   Hortensio will be quit with thee by changing.   *Exit.*

---

71 S.D. *reads* (she intones each line on the note in question) *ground* lowest
note *accord* harmony 78 *nice* capricious 88 *stale* decoy, bait 89 *Seize
. . . list* let him take you that pleases *ranging* straying 90 *changing* i.e.
to another love

Enter Baptista, Gremio, Tranio [as Lucentio], Kate,
   Bianca, [Lucentio as Cambio,] and others (Attendants).

Baptista. *[to Tranio]* Signior Lucentio, this is the 'pointed
      day
   That Katherine and Petruchio should be married,
   And yet we hear not of our son-in-law.
   What will be said? What mockery will it be
   To want the bridegroom when the priest attends   5
   To speak the ceremonial rites of marriage?
   What says Lucentio to this shame of ours?
Kate. No shame but mine. I must, forsooth, be forced
   To give my hand opposed against my heart
   Unto a mad-brain rudesby, full of spleen,   10
   Who wooed in haste and means to wed at leisure.
   I told you, I, he was a frantic fool,
   Hiding his bitter jests in blunt behavior.
   And to be noted for a merry man,
   He'll woo a thousand, 'point the day of marriage,   15
   Make friends, invite, and proclaim the banns,
   Yet never means to wed where he hath wooed.
   Now must the world point at poor Katherine
   And say, 'Lo, there is mad Petruchio's wife,
   If it would please him come and marry her.'   20
Tranio. Patience, good Katherine, and Baptista too.
   Upon my life, Petruchio means but well,
   Whatever fortune stays him from his word.
   Though he be blunt, I know him passing wise;
   Though he be merry, yet withal he's honest.   25
Kate. Would Katherine had never seen him though!
                              Exit weeping [with Bianca].
Baptista. Go, girl, I cannot blame thee now to weep,

III, ii, 8 *forsooth* indeed   10 *rudesby* boor   *spleen* capriciousness   14 *noted
for* known as   25 *withal* at the same time

For such an injury would vex a very saint,
Much more a shrew of thy impatient humor.

Enter Biondello.

30 *Biondello.* Master, master, old news! And such news as you
never heard of!
Baptista. Is it new and old too? How may that be?
Biondello. Why, is it not news to hear of Petruchio's coming?
35 *Baptista.* Is he come?
Biondello. Why, no, sir.
Baptista. What then?
Biondello. He is coming.
Baptista. When will he be here?
40 *Biondello.* When he stands where I am and sees you there.
Tranio. But say, what to thine old news?
Biondello. Why, Petruchio is coming, in a new hat and an
old jerkin; a pair of old breeches thrice turned; a pair of
boots that have been candle-cases, one buckled, another
45 laced; an old rusty sword ta'en out of the town armory,
with a broken hilt and chapeless; with two broken
points; his horse hipped — with an old mothy saddle and
stirrups of no kindred — besides, possessed with the
glanders and like to mose in the chine; troubled with the
50 lampass, infected with the fashions, full of windgalls, sped
with spavins, rayed with the yellows, past cure of the
fives, stark spoiled with the staggers, begnawn with the

29 *humor* disposition 30 *old* great, rare (Baptista misunderstands) 41 *to*
about 43 *jerkin* jacket 44 *candle-cases* (worn-out boots were sometimes
hung on the wall to hold candle-ends and the like) 46 *chapeless* without
the metal plate on the scabbard covering the sword-point 47 *points*
tagged laces for tying hose to doublet *hipped* lamed in the hip 49 *glanders*
disease affecting nose and mouth *mose . . . chine* suffer from glanders
50 *lampass* infected mouth *fashions* disease like glanders *windgalls* leg
tumors 51 *spavins* joint-swellings *yellows* jaundice 52 *fives* swelling
behind the ears *staggers* a kind of palsy

bots, swayed in the back, and shoulder-shotten; near-
legged before, and with a half-cheeked bit and a head-
stall of sheep's leather which, being restrained to keep   55
him from stumbling, hath been often burst and now re-
paired with knots; one girth six times pieced, and a
woman's crupper of velure which hath two letters for her
name, fairly set down in studs, and here and there pieced
with packthread.   60

Baptista. Who comes with him?

Biondello. O sir, his lackey, for all the world caparisoned
like the horse: with a linen stock on one leg and a kersey
boot-hose on the other, gart'red with a red and blue list;
an old hat and the humor of forty fancies pricked in 't for   65
a feather — a monster, a very monster in apparel, and not
like a Christian footboy or a gentleman's lackey.

Tranio. 'Tis some odd humor pricks him to this fashion,
Yet oftentimes he goes but mean-apparelled.

Baptista. I am glad he's come, howsoe'er he comes.   70

Biondello. Why, sir, he comes not.

Baptista. Didst thou not say he comes?

Biondello. Who? That Petruchio came?

Baptista. Ay, that Petruchio came.

Biondello. No, sir, I say his horse comes, with him on his   75
back.

Baptista. Why, that's all one.

53 *bots* stomach worms   *shoulder-shotten* with dislocated shoulder   53–54
near-legged knock-kneed   54 *half-cheeked* with bridle attached half-way up
the *cheek* or side-piece of bit (thus giving inadequate leverage)   54–55
head-stall part of bridle going round the head   55 *sheep's leather* (inferior
to pigskin)   *restrained* drawn back   57 *pieced* patched   58 *crupper* strap
passing under the tail to keep the saddle from working forward   *velure*
velvet   59 *pieced* tied together   63–64 *kersey boot-hose* coarse woollen over-
stocking   64 *list* strip of waste cloth   65 *humor . . . fancies* (meaning
doubtful; some kind of fantastic ornament)   *pricked* pinned   67 *footboy*
liveried attendant   68 *humor* whim   *pricks* spurs, drives   77 *all one* the
same thing

Biondello. *[sings]* Nay, by Saint Jamy,
            I hold you a penny,
80   A horse and a man
            Is more than one
            And yet not many.

Enter Petruchio and Grumio.

Petruchio. Come, where be these gallants? Who's at home?
Baptista. You are welcome, sir.
Petruchio.   And yet I come not well.
85 *Baptista.* And yet you halt not.
Tranio. Not so well apparelled as I wish you were.
Petruchio. Were it better, I should rush in thus.
    But where is Kate? Where is my lovely bride?
    How does my father? Gentles, methinks you frown.
90   And wherefore gaze this goodly company
    As if they saw some wondrous monument,
    Some comet or unusual prodigy?
Baptista. Why, sir, you know this is your wedding-day.
    First were we sad, fearing you would not come,
95   Now sadder that you come so unprovided.
    Fie, doff this habit, shame to your estate,
    An eyesore to our solemn festival.
Tranio. And tell us what occasion of import
    Hath all so long detained you from your wife
100   And sent you hither so unlike yourself?
Petruchio. Tedious it were to tell and harsh to hear.
    Sufficeth I am come to keep my word,
    Though in some part enforcèd to digress,

79 *hold* bet   85 *halt* limp (Baptista quibbles on *come* in the sense of 'walk')
87 *it* i.e. my apparel   92 *prodigy* unnatural phenomenon   95 *unprovided*
improperly equipped   96 *estate* social position   103 *digress* deviate (from
his intention to dress well; cf. II, i, 317)

Which at more leisure I will so excuse
As you shall well be satisfied withal.   105
But where is Kate? I stay too long from her.
The morning wears, 'tis time we were at church.
Tranio. See not your bride in these unreverent robes.
   Go to my chamber; put on clothes of mine.
Petruchio. Not I, believe me. Thus I'll visit her.   110
Baptista. But thus, I trust, you will not marry her?
Petruchio. Good sooth, even thus. Therefore ha' done with
      words.
   To me she's married, not unto my clothes.
   Could I repair what she will wear in me
   As I can change these poor accoutrements,   115
   'Twere well for Kate and better for myself.
   But what a fool am I to chat with you
   When I should bid good morrow to my bride
   And seal the title with a lovely kiss.
                                       Exit [with Grumio].
Tranio. He hath some meaning in his mad attire.   120
   We will persuade him, be it possible,
   To put on better ere he go to church.
Baptista. I'll after him and see the event of this.
                            Exit [with Gremio and Attendants].
Tranio. But sir, to love concerneth us to add
   Her father's liking, which to bring to pass,   125
   As I before imparted to your worship,
   I am to get a man – whate'er he be
   It skills not much, we'll fit him to our turn –
   And he shall be Vincentio of Pisa,

---

105 *withal* with   112 *Good sooth* indeed   114 *wear* wear out   118 *bid . . .*
bride (on the wedding morning it was customary for the groom to awaken
the bride)   119 *seal the title* confirm my rights   *lovely* loving   123 *event*
outcome   128 *skills* matters   *turn* purpose

130   And make assurance here in Padua
       Of greater sums than I have promisèd.
       So shall you quietly enjoy your hope
       And marry sweet Bianca with consent.
    Lucentio. Were it not that my fellow-schoolmaster
135   Doth watch Bianca's steps so narrowly,
       'Twere good, methinks, to steal our marriage,
       Which once performed, let all the world say no,
       I'll keep mine own despite of all the world.
    Tranio. That by degrees we mean to look into
140   And watch our vantage in this business.
       We'll over-reach the greybeard, Gremio,
       The narrow-prying father, Minola,
       The quaint musician, amorous Litio –
       All for my master's sake, Lucentio.

                     Enter Gremio.

145   Signior Gremio, came you from the church?
    Gremio. As willingly as e'er I came from school.
    Tranio. And is the bride and bridegroom coming home?
    Gremio. A bridegroom, say you? 'Tis a groom indeed,
       A grumbling groom, and that the girl shall find.
150 *Tranio.* Curster than she? Why, 'tis impossible.
    Gremio. Why, he's a devil, a devil, a very fiend.
    Tranio. Why, she's a devil, a devil, the devil's dam.
    Gremio. Tut, she's a lamb, a dove, a fool to him.
       I'll tell you, Sir Lucentio. When the priest
155   Should ask if Katherine should be his wife,
       'Ay, by gogs-wouns,' quoth he, and swore so loud

130 *assurance* guarantee   136 *steal our marriage* i.e. marry secretly   143
quaint clever   148 *groom* (quibbling on 'servant,' rough-mannered fellow)
152 *dam* mother   153 *to* compared with   156 *by gogs-wouns* by God's
(Christ's) wounds

That, all amazed, the priest let fall the book,
And as he stooped again to take it up
This mad-brained bridegroom took him such a cuff
That down fell priest and book, and book and priest.   160
'Now, take them up,' quoth he, 'if any list.'
Tranio. What said the wench when he rose again?
Gremio. Trembled and shook, forwhy he stamped and
     swore,
As if the vicar meant to cozen him.
But after many ceremonies done   165
He calls for wine. 'A health!' quoth he, as if
He had been aboard, carousing to his mates
After a storm; quaffed off the muscadel
And threw the sops all in the sexton's face,
Having no other reason   170
But that his beard grew thin and hungerly
And seemed to ask him sops as he was drinking.
This done, he took the bride about the neck
And kissed her lips with such a clamorous smack
That at the parting all the church did echo.   175
And I, seeing this, came thence for very shame,
And after me, I know, the rout is coming.
Such a mad marriage never was before.
Hark, hark, I hear the minstrels play.   *Music plays.*

Enter Petruchio, Kate, Bianca, Hortensio [as Litio],
    Baptista, [Grumio, and Attendants].

Petruchio. Gentlemen and friends, I thank you for your
     pains.   180

159 *took* gave   161 *if any list* if anyone pleases   163 *forwhy* because
164 *cozen* cheat (with an invalid ceremony)   168 *muscadel* a sweet wine
(to be avoided by persons of choleric disposition)   169 *sops* dregs   171
hungerly sparsely   172 *ask him* ask him for   *sops* pieces of cake soaked in
wine   177 *rout* mob

I know you think to dine with me to-day
And have prepared great store of wedding cheer,
But so it is, my haste doth call me hence
And therefore here I mean to take my leave.

185 *Baptista.* Is't possible you will away to-night?
Petruchio. I must away to-day, before night come.
Make it no wonder. If you knew my business
You would entreat me rather go than stay.
And, honest company, I thank you all,

190 That have beheld me give away myself
To this most patient, sweet, and virtuous wife.
Dine with my father, drink a health to me,
For I must hence; and farewell to you all.
Tranio. Let us entreat you stay till after dinner.
Petruchio. It may not be.

195 *Gremio.*   Let me entreat you.
Petruchio. It cannot be.
Kate.   Let me entreat you.
Petruchio. I am content.
Kate.   Are you content to stay?
Petruchio. I am content you shall entreat me stay,
But yet not stay, entreat me how you can.
Kate. Now if you love me, stay.

200 *Petruchio.*   Grumio, my horse!
Grumio. Ay, sir, they be ready; the oats have eaten the
horses.
Kate. Nay then,
Do what thou canst, I will not go to-day,

205 No, nor to-morrow, not till I please myself.
The door is open, sir, there lies your way;

---

182 *cheer* entertainment   187 *Make* consider   200 *horse* horses (old
plural)   201-2 *the oats . . . horses* (Grumio gets it backwards)

90

You may be jogging whiles your boots are green.
For me, I'll not be gone till I please myself.
'Tis like you'll prove a jolly surly groom,
That take it on you at the first so roundly.   210
Petruchio. O Kate, content thee; prithee, be not angry.
Kate. I will be angry. What hast thou to do?
Father, be quiet, he shall stay my leisure.
Gremio. Ay, marry, sir, now it begins to work.
Kate. Gentlemen, forward to the bridal dinner.   215
I see a woman may be made a fool
If she had not a spirit to resist.
Petruchio. They shall go forward, Kate, at thy command.
Obey the bride, you that attend on her,
Go to the feast, revel and domineer,   220
Carouse full measure to her maidenhead,
Be mad and merry or go hang yourselves.
But for my bonny Kate, she must with me.
Nay, look not big, nor stamp, nor stare, nor fret;
I will be master of what is mine own.   225
She is my goods, my chattels; she is my house,
My household stuff, my field, my barn,
My horse, my ox, my ass, my anything;
And here she stands, touch her whoever dare.
I'll bring mine action on the proudest he   230
That stops my way in Padua. Grumio,
Draw forth thy weapon, we are beset with thieves.
Rescue thy mistress, if thou be a man.

---

207 *You may . . . green* (proverbial for getting an early start) *green* i.e.
fresh 209 *jolly* arrogant 210 *take it on you* assert yourself *roundly* un-
ceremoniously 211 *prithee* I pray thee 212 *What . . . do* what business is
it of yours 220 *domineer* carouse 224 *big* threatening 226–28 *my house
. . . ass* (echoing the Tenth Commandment, 'Thou shalt not covet thy
neighbor's house, nor his ox, nor his ass') 230 *action* lawsuit

Fear not, sweet wench; they shall not touch thee, Kate.
235   I'll buckler thee against a million.

                     Exeunt Petruchio, Kate, [and Grumio].

Baptista. Nay, let them go, a couple of quiet ones.

Gremio. Went they not quickly, I should die with laughing.

Tranio. Of all mad matches never was the like.

Lucentio. Mistress, what's your opinion of your sister?

240 *Bianca.* That being mad herself, she's madly mated.

Gremio. I warrant him, Petruchio is Kated.

Baptista. Neighbors and friends, though bride and bride-
    groom wants
    For to supply the places at the table,
    You know there wants no junkets at the feast.

245 Lucentio, you shall supply the bridegroom's place,
    And let Bianca take her sister's room.

Tranio. Shall sweet Bianca practice how to bride it?

Baptista. She shall, Lucentio. Come, gentlemen, let's go.

                              Exeunt.

                      Enter Grumio.

Grumio. Fie, fie, on all tired jades, on all mad masters, and
    all foul ways! Was ever man so beaten? Was ever man
    so rayed? Was ever man so weary? I am sent before to
    make a fire, and they are coming after to warm them.
5   Now were not I a little pot and soon hot, my very lips
    might freeze to my teeth, my tongue to the roof of my
    mouth, my heart in my belly, ere I should come by a

---

235 *buckler* shield 244 *junkets* delicacies IV, i, 1 *jades* worthless horses
2 *ways* roads 3 *rayed* dirtied 5 *a little . . . hot* (proverbial of a small
person easily angered)

fire to thaw me. But I with blowing the fire shall warm myself, for considering the weather, a taller man than I will take cold. Holla, ho! Curtis. 10

Enter Curtis (a Servant).

Curtis. Who is't that calls so coldly?

Grumio. A piece of ice. If thou doubt it, thou mayst slide from my shoulder to my heel with no greater a run but my head and my neck. A fire, good Curtis.

Curtis. Is my master and his wife coming, Grumio? 15

Grumio. O ay, Curtis, ay, and therefore fire, fire; cast on no water.

Curtis. Is she so hot a shrew as she's reported?

Grumio. She was, good Curtis, before this frost. But thou know'st winter tames man, woman, and beast, for it hath 20 tamed my old master and my new mistress and myself, fellow Curtis.

Curtis. Away, you three-inch fool! I am no beast.

Grumio. Am I but three inches? Why, thy horn is a foot, and so long am I at the least. But wilt thou make a fire or 25 shall I complain on thee to our mistress, whose hand – she being now at hand – thou shalt soon feel, to thy cold comfort, for being slow in thy hot office?

Curtis. I prithee, good Grumio, tell me, how goes the world? 30

Grumio. A cold world, Curtis, in every office but thine, and therefore fire. Do thy duty, and have thy duty, for my master and mistress are almost frozen to death.

---

9 *taller* (playing on 'better') 16–17 *cast on no water* (Grumio misquotes from the round, 'Scotland's Burning') 23 *three-inch* i.e. very short *I am no beast* (Grumio having called himself a *beast* and Curtis his *fellow*) 24 *horn* i.e. of a cuckold 28 *hot office* task of providing heat 32 *have thy duty* have thy due, reward (proverbial)

Curtis. There's fire ready, and therefore, good Grumio,
35   the news.

Grumio. Why, *[sings]* 'Jack boy, ho boy,' and as much
news as thou wilt.

Curtis. Come, you are so full of cony-catching.

Grumio. Why therefore fire, for I have caught extreme
40   cold. Where's the cook? Is supper ready, the house
trimmed, rushes strewed, cobwebs swept, the servingmen
in their new fustian, the white stockings, and every officer
his wedding-garment on? Be the jacks fair within, the
jills fair without, the carpets laid, and everything in order?

45 *Curtis.* All ready, and therefore, I pray thee, news.

Grumio. First, know my horse is tired, my master and
mistress fall'n out.

Curtis. How?

Grumio. Out of their saddles into the dirt — and thereby
50   hangs a tale.

Curtis. Let's ha't, good Grumio.

Grumio. Lend thine ear.

Curtis. Here.

Grumio. There.   *[Strikes him.]*

55 *Curtis.* This 'tis to feel a tale, not to hear a tale.

Grumio. And therefore 'tis called a sensible tale, and this
cuff was but to knock at your ear and beseech listening.
Now I begin. Imprimis, we came down a foul hill, my
master riding behind my mistress —

60 *Curtis.* Both of one horse?

---

38 *cony-catching* trickery (a *cony* being a rabbit; with a play on *Jack boy, ho boy,* a 'catch' or round)   41 *rushes strewed* i.e. on the floor   42 *fustian* coarse cotton cloth   43 *jacks* leather drinking vessels (playing on 'fellows,' servingmen)   44 *jills* metal measuring cups (playing on 'girls,' maid-servants)   *carpets* table-covers   56 *sensible* (playing on 'capable of being felt')   58 *Imprimis* first   60 *of* on

Grumio. What's that to thee?

Curtis. Why, a horse.

Grumio. Tell thou the tale — but hadst thou not crossed me thou shouldst have heard how her horse fell, and she under her horse; thou shouldst have heard in how miry 65 a place; how she was bemoiled, how he left her with the horse upon her, how he beat me because her horse stumbled, how she waded through the dirt to pluck him off me; how he swore, how she prayed, that never prayed before; how I cried, how the horses ran away, how her 70 bridle was burst; how I lost my crupper — with many things of worthy memory, which now shall die in oblivion, and thou return unexperienced to thy grave

Curtis. By this reck'ning he is more shrew than she.

Grumio. Ay, and that thou and the proudest of you all shall 75 find when he comes home. But what talk I of this? Call forth Nathaniel, Joseph, Nicholas, Philip, Walter, Sugarsop, and the rest. Let their heads be sleekly combed, their blue coats brushed, and their garters of an indifferent knit. Let them curtsy with their left legs and not presume 80 to touch a hair of my master's horsetail till they kiss their hands. Are they all ready?

Curtis. They are.

Grumio. Call them forth.

Curtis. Do you hear, ho! You must meet my master to 85 countenance my mistress.

Grumio. Why, she hath a face of her own.

Curtis. Who knows not that?

---

63 *crossed* interrupted   66 *bemoiled* bemired   73 *unexperienced* (hence ignorant)   76 *what* why   79 *blue coats* (dark blue was the usual color of a servant's dress)   *indifferent* not different, the same, matching   86 *countenance* do honor to (Grumio quibbles on 'face')

Grumio. Thou, it seems, that calls for company to counte-
90 nance her.

Curtis. I call them forth to credit her.

Enter four or five Servingmen.

Grumio. Why, she comes to borrow nothing of them.

Nathaniel. Welcome home, Grumio!

Philip. How now, Grumio?

95 *Joseph.* What, Grumio!

Nicholas. Fellow Grumio!

Nathaniel. How now, old lad!

Grumio. Welcome, you; how now, you; what, you; fellow, you; and thus much for greeting. Now, my spruce
100 companions, is all ready and all things neat?

Nathaniel. All things is ready. How near is our master?

Grumio. E'en at hand, alighted by this. And therefore be
not — Cock's passion, silence, I hear my master.

Enter Petruchio and Kate.

Petruchio. Where be these knaves? What, no man at door
105 To hold my stirrup nor to take my horse?
Where is Nathaniel, Gregory, Philip?

All Servingmen. Here, here, sir; here, sir.

Petruchio. Here, sir; here, sir; here, sir; here, sir!
You loggerheaded and unpolished grooms!
110 What, no attendance? No regard? No duty?
Where is the foolish knave I sent before?

Grumio. Here, sir, as foolish as I was before.

Petruchio. You peasant swain, you whoreson malt-horse
drudge!

91 *credit* pay respect to (Grumio quibbles) 103 *Cock's passion* by God's
(Christ's) suffering 113 *swain* lout *whoreson* contemptible *malt-horse
drudge* brewer's horse which ploddingly turns a grain mill

Did I not bid thee meet me in the park
    And bring along these rascal knaves with thee?   115
Grumio. Nathaniel's coat, sir, was not fully made,
    And Gabriel's pumps were all unpinked i' th' heel.
    There was no link to color Peter's hat,
    And Walter's dagger was not come from sheathing.
    There were none fine but Adam, Rafe, and Gregory;   120
    The rest were ragged, old, and beggarly.
    Yet, as they are, here are they come to meet you.
Petruchio. Go, rascals, go, and fetch my supper in.

                                        Exeunt Servants.

[Sings] 'Where is the life that late I led?'
    Where are those — ? Sit down, Kate, *[They sit at table.]*   125
    And welcome. Food, food, food, food!

                Enter Servants with supper.

Why, when, I say? — Nay, good sweet Kate, be merry.
    Off with my boots, you rogues! You villains, when?
    [Sings] 'It was the friar of orders grey,
            As he forth walkèd on his way' —   130
    Out, you rogue! You pluck my foot awry.

                                        [Strikes him.]
    Take that, and mend the plucking off the other.
    Be merry, Kate. Some water here, what ho!

                Enter one with water.

Where's my spaniel Troilus? Sirrah, get you hence
    And bid my cousin Ferdinand come hither —   135

                                        [Exit Servant.]

---

114 *park* enclosed tract of land stocked with game   117 *unpinked* without
ornamental pattern punched or cut in the leather   118 *link* torch (the
smoke being used to blacken hats)   120 *fine* well turned out   125 *those*
i.e. the servants

One, Kate, that you must kiss and be acquainted with.
Where are my slippers? Shall I have some water?
Come, Kate, and wash, and welcome heartily.
You whoreson villain, will you let it fall? *[Strikes him.]*
140 *Kate.* Patience, I pray you, 'twas a fault unwilling.
Petruchio. A whoreson, beetle-headed, flap-eared knave!
Come, Kate, sit down; I know you have a stomach.
Will you give thanks, sweet Kate, or else shall I?
What's this, mutton?
145 *1. Servant.* Ay.
Petruchio. Who brought it?
Peter. I.
Petruchio. 'Tis burnt, and so is all the meat.
What dogs are these! Where is the rascal cook?
150 How durst you, villains, bring it from the dresser,
And serve it thus to me that love it not?
                              [He throws it at them.]
There, take it to you, trenchers, cups, and all.
You heedless joltheads and unmannered slaves!
What, do you grumble? I'll be with you straight.
                              [Exeunt Servants.]
155 *Kate.* I pray you, husband, be not so disquiet.
The meat was well if you were so contented.
Petruchio. I tell thee, Kate, 'twas burnt and dried away,
And I expressly am forbid to touch it,
For it engenders choler, planteth anger,
160 And better 'twere that both of us did fast,
Since of ourselves, ourselves are choleric,

141 *beetle-headed* blockheaded, stupid (the *head* of a *beetle*, the pounding tool, being usually a heavy block of wood) 142 *stomach* appetite (playing on 'temper') 143 *give thanks* i.e. say grace 145 *1. Servant* (Curtis or Peter) 150 *dresser* sideboard 152 *trenchers* wooden plates 154 *with you* even with you 159 *choler* that 'humor' (hot and dry) which produces anger (roast meat was to be avoided by persons of such disposition)

Than feed it with such over-roasted flesh.
Be patient. To-morrow't shall be mended,
And for this night we'll fast for company.
Come, I will bring thee to thy bridal chamber. *Exeunt.* 165

Enter Servants severally.

Nathaniel. Peter, didst ever see the like?
Peter. He kills her in her own humor.

Enter Curtis.

Grumio. Where is he?
Curtis. In her chamber, making a sermon of continency to
her,   170
And rails and swears and rates, that she, poor soul,
Knows not which way to stand, to look, to speak,
And sits as one new-risen from a dream.
Away, away, for he is coming hither.   *[Exeunt.]*

Enter Petruchio.

Petruchio. Thus have I politicly begun my reign,   175
And 'tis my hope to end successfully.
My falcon now is sharp and passing empty,
And till she stoop she must not be full-gorged,
For then she never looks upon her lure.
Another way I have to man my haggard,   180
To make her come and know her keeper's call:
That is, to watch her as we watch these kites

162 *it* i.e. their choler 165 s.d. *severally* at different doors 167 *kills . . .
humor* subdues her by displaying the same disposition as hers 171 *rates*
berates 175 *politicly* cunningly 177 *sharp* starved 178 *stoop* fly to and
seize the lure (playing on 'bow to authority') 179 *lure* feathered wicker
container swung up into the air by the falconer to recall a hawk 180 *man*
tame (hawking term, with a quibble) *haggard* wild female hawk 182
watch keep awake (as in taming a wild hawk) *kites* inferior hawks

That bate and beat and will not be obedient.
She eat no meat to-day, nor none shall eat.
185 Last night she slept not, nor to-night she shall not.
As with the meat, some undeservèd fault
I'll find about the making of the bed,
And here I'll fling the pillow, there the bolster,
This way the coverlet, another way the sheets.
190 Ay, and amid this hurly I intend
That all is done in reverent care of her.
And in conclusion she shall watch all night,
And if she chance to nod I'll rail and brawl
And with the clamor keep her still awake.
195 This is a way to kill a wife with kindness,
And thus I'll curb her mad and headstrong humor.
He that knows better how to tame a shrow,
Now let him speak: 'tis charity to show.   *Exit.*

IV, ii   *Enter Tranio [as Lucentio] and Hortensio [as Litio].*

Tranio. Is't possible, friend Litio, that Mistress Bianca
Doth fancy any other but Lucentio?
I tell you, sir, she bears me fair in hand.
Hortensio. Sir, to satisfy you in what I have said,
5   Stand by and mark the manner of his teaching.
                        [They stand aside.]

183 *bate and beat* flutter and flap the wings   184 *She eat* she ate (pronounced *et*)   188 *bolster* long narrow cushion supporting the pillow
190 *intend* pretend   195 *kill . . . kindness* (ironically, referring to the
proverb for spoiling a wife through overindulgence)   196 *humor* disposition   197 *shrow* (the pronunciation indicated by the rhyme was the normal
one)   IV, ii, 3 *bears . . . hand* encourages me

Enter Bianca [and Lucentio as Cambio].

Lucentio. Now mistress, profit you in what you read?

Bianca. What, master, read you? First resolve me that.

Lucentio. I read that I profess, the Art to Love.

Bianca. And may you prove, sir, master of your art.

Lucentio. While you, sweet dear, prove mistress of my
     heart.   *[They stand aside.]* 10

Hortensio. *[advancing]* Quick proceeders, marry! Now tell
    me, I pray,

  You that durst swear that your mistress Bianca

  Loved none in the world so well as Lucentio.

Tranio. O despiteful love, unconstant womankind!

  I tell thee, Litio, this is wonderful.   15

Hortensio. Mistake no more: I am not Litio,

  Nor a musician, as I seem to be,

  But one that scorn to live in this disguise,

  For such a one as leaves a gentleman

  And makes a god of such a cullion.   20

  Know, sir, that I am called Hortensio.

Tranio. Signior Hortensio, I have often heard

  Of your entire affection to Bianca,

  And since mine eyes are witness of her lightness

  I will, with you, if you be so contented,   25

  Forswear Bianca and her love forever.

Hortensio. See how they kiss and court. Signior Lucentio,

  Here is my hand and here I firmly vow

  Never to woo her more, but do forswear her,

---

6 *read* study   7 *resolve* answer   8 *the Art to Love* (Ovid's *Ars amatoria*)
11 *proceeders* candidates for a degree (playing on *master of your art*)   *marry*
indeed (originally an oath by the Virgin Mary)   14 *despiteful* spiteful
15 *wonderful* i.e. a source of wonder   20 *cullion* base fellow   24 *lightness*
wantonness   26 *Forswear* swear to renounce

30   As one unworthy all the former favors
        That I have fondly flattered her withal.
    Tranio. And here I take the like unfeignèd oath,
        Never to marry with her though she would entreat.
        Fie on her, see how beastly she doth court him.
35 *Hortensio.* Would all the world but he had quite forsworn.
        For me, that I may surely keep mine oath,
        I will be married to a wealthy widow
        Ere three days pass, which hath as long loved me
        As I have loved this proud disdainful haggard.
40   And so farewell, Signior Lucentio.
        Kindness in women, not their beauteous looks,
        Shall win my love — and so I take my leave,
        In resolution as I swore before.   *[Exit.]*
    Tranio. Mistress Bianca, bless you with such grace
45   As 'longeth to a lover's blessed case.
        Nay, I have ta'en you napping, gentle love,
        And have forsworn you with Hortensio.
    Bianca. [advancing] Tranio, you jest. But have you both
        forsworn me?
    Tranio. Mistress, we have.
    Lucentio.   Then we are rid of Litio.
50 *Tranio.* I' faith, he'll have a lusty widow now,
        That shall be wooed and wedded in a day.
    Bianca. God give him joy.
    Tranio. Ay, and he'll tame her.
    Bianca.   He says so, Tranio.
    Tranio. Faith, he is gone unto the taming-school.
55 *Bianca.* The taming-school? What, is there such a
        place?
    Tranio. Ay, mistress, and Petruchio is the master,

31 *fondly* foolishly   34 *beastly* lasciviously   39 *haggard* wild female hawk
50 *lusty* merry

That teacheth tricks eleven and twenty long
To tame a shrew and charm her chattering tongue.

Enter Biondello.

Biondello. O master, master, I have watched so long
  That I am dog-weary, but at last I spied   60
  An ancient angel coming down the hill
  Will serve the turn.
Tranio.   What is he, Biondello?
Biondello. Master, a mercatante or a pedant,
  I know not what; but formal in apparel,
  In gait and countenance surely like a father.   65
Lucentio. And what of him, Tranio?
Tranio. If he be credulous and trust my tale
  I'll make him glad to seem Vincentio,
  And give assurance to Baptista Minola
  As if he were the right Vincentio.   70
  Take in your love and then let me alone.
             [Exeunt Lucentio and Bianca.]

Enter a Pedant.

Pedant. God save you, sir.
Tranio.   And you, sir. You are welcome.
  Travel you far on, or are you at the farthest?
Pedant. Sir, at the farthest for a week or two,
  But then up farther and as far as Rome,   75
  And so to Tripoli, if God lend me life.
Tranio. What countryman, I pray?

57 *eleven . . . long* i.e. a great many (referring to the card-game of one and
thirty) 61 *angel* fellow of the good old stamp (an *angel* being a gold
coin) 62 *the turn* our purposes 63 *mercatante* merchant (the Pedant is
actually a merchant, as is shown by his intention of delivering bills of
exchange in Padua, ll. 89–90) *pedant* schoolmaster 65 *countenance* appearance 73 *at the farthest* i.e. at your destination

Pedant.   Of Mantua.

Tranio. Of Mantua, sir? Marry, God forbid!
     And come to Padua, careless of your life?

80 *Pedant.* My life, sir? How, I pray? For that goes hard.

Tranio. 'Tis death for anyone in Mantua
     To come to Padua. Know you not the cause?
     Your ships are stayed at Venice, and the Duke —
     For private quarrel 'twixt your Duke and him —

85   Hath published and proclaimed it openly.
     'Tis marvel, but that you are but newly come,
     You might have heard it else proclaimed about.

Pedant. Alas, sir, it is worse for me than so,
     For I have bills for money by exchange

90   From Florence and must here deliver them.

Tranio. Well, sir, to do you courtesy,
     This will I do and this I will advise you —
     First, tell me, have you ever been at Pisa?

Pedant. Ay, sir, in Pisa have I often been,

95   Pisa, renownèd for grave citizens.

Tranio. Among them, know you one Vincentio?

Pedant. I know him not but I have heard of him,
     A merchant of incomparable wealth.

Tranio. He is my father, sir, and sooth to say,

100 In count'nance somewhat doth resemble you.

Biondello. [aside] As much as an apple doth an oyster, and
     all one.

Tranio. To save your life in this extremity
     This favor will I do you for his sake,

105 And think it not the worst of all your fortunes
     That you are like to Sir Vincentio.
     His name and credit shall you undertake,

80 *goes hard* is serious   102 *all one* the same thing   107 *credit* reputation
undertake assume

And in my house you shall be friendly lodged.
Look that you take upon you as you should.
You understand me, sir. So shall you stay   110
Till you have done your business in the city.
If this be court'sy, sir, accept of it.
Pedant. O sir, I do, and will repute you ever
  The patron of my life and liberty.
Tranio. Then go with me to make the matter good.   115
  This, by the way, I let you understand.
  My father is here looked for every day
  To pass assurance of a dower in marriage
  'Twixt me and one Baptista's daughter here.
  In all these circumstances I'll instruct you.   120
  Go with me to clothe you as becomes you.   *Exeunt.*

Enter Kate and Grumio.   IV, iii

Grumio. No, no, forsooth, I dare not for my life.
Kate. The more my wrong, the more his spite appears.
  What, did he marry me to famish me?
  Beggars that come unto my father's door,
  Upon entreaty have a present alms;   5
  If not, elsewhere they meet with charity.
  But I, who never knew how to entreat
  Nor never needed that I should entreat,
  Am starved for meat, giddy for lack of sleep,
  With oaths kept waking and with brawling fed.   10

---

109 *take upon you* play your part   116 *by the way* along the way, as we go
118 *pass* convey (legal term)   *assurance* a guarantee   IV, iii, 2 *my wrong*
i.e. the wrong done me   5 *present* immediate   9 *meat* food

And that which spites me more than all these wants,
He does it under name of perfect love,
As who should say, if I should sleep or eat
'Twere deadly sickness or else present death.

15 I prithee go and get me some repast,
I care not what, so it be wholesome food.

Grumio. What say you to a neat's foot?

Kate. 'Tis passing good, I prithee let me have it.

Grumio. I fear it is too choleric a meat.

20 How say you to a fat tripe finely broiled?

Kate. I like it well, good Grumio, fetch it me.

Grumio. I cannot tell; I fear 'tis choleric.
What say you to a piece of beef and mustard?

Kate. A dish that I do love to feed upon.

25 *Grumio.* Ay, but the mustard is too hot a little.

Kate. Why then, the beef, and let the mustard rest.

Grumio. Nay then, I will not; you shall have the mustard
Or else you get no beef of Grumio.

Kate. Then both or one, or anything thou wilt.

30 *Grumio.* Why then, the mustard without the beef.

Kate. Go, get thee gone, thou false deluding slave,

Beats him.

That feed'st me with the very name of meat.
Sorrow on thee and all the pack of you
That triumph thus upon my misery.

35 Go, get thee gone, I say.

Enter Petruchio and Hortensio with meat.

Petruchio. How fares my Kate? What, sweeting, all amort?

13 *As who* as though one 17 *neat's foot* ox's or calf's foot 19 *choleric*
engendering anger (neat's-foot, tripe, and beef, but not mustard, were
recommended for persons of choleric disposition) 32 *very* i.e. mere
36 *sweeting* sweetheart *all amort* spiritless, dejected

Hortensio. Mistress, what cheer?

Kate. Faith, as cold as can be.

Petruchio. Pluck up thy spirits, look cheerfully upon me.
Here, love, thou seest how diligent I am
To dress thy meat myself and bring it thee. 40
I am sure, sweet Kate, this kindness merits thanks.
What, not a word? Nay then, thou lov'st it not,
And all my pains is sorted to no proof.
Here, take away this dish.

Kate. I pray you, let it stand.

Petruchio. The poorest service is repaid with thanks, 45
And so shall mine before you touch the meat.

Kate. I thank you, sir.

Hortensio. Signior Petruchio, fie, you are to blame.
Come, Mistress Kate, I'll bear you company.

[They sit at table.]

Petruchio. [aside] Eat it up all, Hortensio, if thou lov'st me. 50
Much good do it unto thy gentle heart.
Kate, eat apace. And now, my honey love,
Will we return unto thy father's house
And revel it as bravely as the best,
With silken coats and caps and golden rings, 55
With ruffs and cuffs and farthingales and things;
With scarfs and fans and double change of brav'ry,
With amber bracelets, beads, and all this knav'ry.
What, hast thou dined? The tailor stays thy leisure,
To deck thy body with his ruffling treasure. 60

Enter Tailor [with a gown].

Come, tailor, let us see these ornaments.

---

40 *dress* prepare 43 *is . . . proof* have resulted in nothing 52 *apace* quickly
54 *bravely* finely dressed 56 *farthingales* hooped petticoats 57 *brav'ry*
finery 60 *ruffling* ornamented with ruffles

Enter Haberdasher [with a cap].

Lay forth the gown. — What news with you, sir?
Haberdasher. Here is the cap your worship did bespeak.
Petruchio. Why, this was molded on a porringer:
65 A velvet dish. Fie, fie, 'tis lewd and filthy.
Why, 'tis a cockle or a walnut shell,
A knack, a toy, a trick, a baby's cap.
Away with it. Come, let me have a bigger.
Kate. I'll have no bigger, this doth fit the time,
70 And gentlewomen wear such caps as these.
Petruchio. When you are gentle you shall have one too,
And not till then.
Hortensio. [aside]   That will not be in haste.
Kate. Why, sir, I trust I may have leave to speak,
And speak I will. I am no child, no babe.
75 Your betters have endured me say my mind,
And if you cannot, best you stop your ears.
My tongue will tell the anger of my heart
Or else my heart, concealing it, will break,
And rather than it shall, I will be free
80 Even to the uttermost, as I please, in words.
Petruchio. Why, thou sayst true. It is a paltry cap,
A custard-coffin, a bauble, a silken pie.
I love thee well in that thou lik'st it not.
Kate. Love me or love me not, I like the cap,
85 And it I will have or I will have none.

[Exit Haberdasher.]

Petruchio. Thy gown? Why, ay — come, tailor, let us see't.

---

63 *bespeak* order 64 *porringer* bowl for soup or porridge 65 *lewd* vile
66 *cockle* cockleshell 67 *knack* trinket *trick* trifle 69 *fit the time* accord
with present fashion 82 *custard-coffin* custard-crust *pie* i.e. meat-pie
(several inches deep)

O mercy, God, what masquing stuff is here?
What's this, a sleeve? 'Tis like a demi-cannon.
What, up and down carved like an apple tart?
Here's snip and nip and cut and slish and slash,   90
Like to a censer in a barber's shop.
Why, what a devil's name, tailor, call'st thou this?

Hortensio. [aside] I see she's like to have neither cap nor
    gown.

Tailor. You bid me make it orderly and well,
According to the fashion and the time.   95

Petruchio. Marry, and did. But if you be rememb'red,
I did not bid you mar it to the time.
Go, hop me over every kennel home,
For you shall hop without my custom, sir.
I'll none of it. Hence, make your best of it.   100

Kate. I never saw a better-fashioned gown,
More quaint, more pleasing, nor more commendable.
Belike you mean to make a puppet of me.

Petruchio. Why, true, he means to make a puppet of thee.

Tailor. She says your worship means to make a puppet of
    her.   105

Petruchio. O monstrous arrogance!
Thou liest, thou thread, thou thimble,
Thou yard, three-quarters, half-yard, quarter, nail!
Thou flea, thou nit, thou winter-cricket thou!
Braved in mine own house with a skein of thread?   110
Away, thou rag, thou quantity, thou remnant,

---

87 *masquing* i.e. fit for masques   88 *demi-cannon* large cannon   89 *up and down* in every respect, exactly   91 *censer* brazier in which perfume was burned, the fumes rising through a perforated cover   98 *kennel* channel, gutter   102 *quaint* handsome   103 *Belike* likely   *puppet* (contemptuous term for a woman)   108 *nail* 2¼ inches (a measure of length for cloth)   109 *nit* louse's egg   110 *Braved* defied   *with* by   111 *quantity* fragment

Or I shall so bemete thee with thy yard
As thou shalt think on prating whilst thou liv'st.
I tell thee, I, that thou hast marred her gown.

115 *Tailor.* Your worship is deceived. The gown is made
Just as my master had direction.
Grumio gave order how it should be done.

Grumio. I gave him no order, I gave him the stuff.

Tailor. But how did you desire it should be made?

120 *Grumio.* Marry, sir, with needle and thread.

Tailor. But did you not request to have it cut?

Grumio. Thou hast faced many things.

Tailor. I have.

Grumio. Face not me. Thou hast braved many men: brave
125 not me. I will neither be faced nor braved. I say unto thee,
I bid thy master cut out the gown but I did not bid him
cut it to pieces. Ergo, thou liest.

Tailor. Why, here is the note of the fashion to testify.

Petruchio. Read it.

130 *Grumio.* The note lies in's throat if he say I said so.

Tailor. [*reads*] 'Imprimis, a loose-bodied gown –'

Grumio. Master, if ever I said loose-bodied gown, sew me
in the skirts of it and beat me to death with a bottom of
brown thread. I said, a gown.

135 *Petruchio.* Proceed.

Tailor. 'With a small compassed cape –'

Grumio. I confess the cape.

Tailor. 'With a trunk sleeve –'

---

112 *bemete* bemeasure (i.e. beat) *yard* yardstick 113 *think on* consider
carefully before 122 *faced* trimmed (followed by a quibble, in *Face*, on
'bully') 124 *braved* dressed finely (followed by a quibble, in *brave*, on
'defy') 127 *Ergo* therefore 130 *in's throat* foully, infamously *he* it 131
Imprimis first *loose-bodied gown* (sort of dress worn by prostitutes)
133 *bottom* ball 136 *compassed* i.e. with the edge forming a circle 138
trunk i.e. very full

Grumio. I confess two sleeves.

Tailor. 'The sleeves curiously cut.'   140

Petruchio. Ay, there's the villainy.

Grumio. Error i' th' bill, sir, error i' th' bill. I commanded
   the sleeves should be cut out and sewed up again, and
   that I'll prove upon thee, though thy little finger be
   armed in a thimble.   145

Tailor. This is true that I say. An I had thee in place where,
   thou shouldst know it.

Grumio. I am for thee straight. Take thou the bill, give me
   thy mete-yard, and spare not me.

Hortensio. God-a-mercy, Grumio, then he shall have no   150
   odds.

Petruchio. Well, sir, in brief, the gown is not for me.

Grumio. You are i' th' right, sir, 'tis for my mistress.

Petruchio. Go, take it up unto thy master's use.

Grumio. Villain, not for thy life. Take up my mistress'   155
   gown for thy master's use!

Petruchio. Why, sir, what's your conceit in that?

Grumio. O sir, the conceit is deeper than you think for.
   Take up my mistress' gown to his master's use!
   O, fie, fie, fie!   160

Petruchio. [*aside*] Hortensio, say thou wilt see the tailor paid.
   [*To Tailor*] Go take it hence, be gone and say no more.

Hortensio. Tailor, I'll pay thee for thy gown to-morrow.
   Take no unkindness of his hasty words.
   Away, I say. Commend me to thy master.   *Exit Tailor.*   165

Petruchio. Well, come, my Kate; we will unto your father's,
   Even in these honest mean habiliments.

---

140 *curiously* elaborately   144 *prove upon* maintain by fighting with   146
in place where in a fit place   148 *bill* (playing on 'halberd')   149 *mete-yard*
measuring-stick   154 *use* i.e. whatever use he can put it to (but Grumio
quibbles bawdily)   157 *conceit* meaning   167 *habiliments* clothes

Our purses shall be proud, our garments poor,
For 'tis the mind that makes the body rich;
170   And as the sun breaks through the darkest clouds
So honor peereth in the meanest habit.
What, is the jay more precious than the lark
Because his feathers are more beautiful?
Or is the adder better than the eel
175   Because his painted skin contents the eye?
O no, good Kate; neither art thou the worse
For this poor furniture and mean array.
If thou account'st it shame, lay it on me.
And therefore frolic; we will hence forthwith
180   To feast and sport us at thy father's house.
[*To Grumio*] Go call my men, and let us straight to
him;
And bring our horses unto Long-lane end.
There will we mount, and thither walk on foot.
Let's see, I think 'tis now some seven o'clock,
185   And well we may come there by dinnertime.
Kate. I dare assure you, sir, 'tis almost two,
And 'twill be suppertime ere you come there.
Petruchio. It shall be seven ere I go to horse.
Look what I speak or do or think to do,
190   You are still crossing it. Sirs, let 't alone.
I will not go to-day, and ere I do,
It shall be what o'clock I say it is.
Hortensio. Why, so this gallant will command the sun.
[*Exeunt.*]

171 *peereth* is seen   *habit* dress   177 *furniture* clothing   179 *hence* i.e. go
hence   *forthwith* immediately   185 *dinnertime* about noon   189 *Look
what* whatever

*Enter Tranio [as Lucentio] and the Pedant booted and
    dressed like Vincentio.*

Tranio. Sir, this is the house. Please it you that I call?
Pedant. Ay, what else? And but I be deceived,
    Signior Baptista may remember me,
    Near twenty years ago, in Genoa,
    Where we were lodgers at the Pegasus.   5
Tranio. 'Tis well, and hold your own in any case
    With such austerity as longeth to a father.

Enter Biondello.

Pedant. I warrant you. But sir, here comes your boy;
    'Twere good he were schooled.
Tranio. Fear you not him. Sirrah Biondello,   10
    Now do your duty throughly, I advise you.
    Imagine 'twere the right Vincentio.
Biondello. Tut, fear not me.
Tranio. But hast thou done thy errand to Baptista?
Biondello. I told him that your father was at Venice,   15
    And that you looked for him this day in Padua.
Tranio. Th'art a tall fellow. Hold thee that to drink.
                                        [Gives money.]
    Here comes Baptista. Set your countenance, sir.

*Enter Baptista and Lucentio [as Cambio]. Pedant bare-
    headed.*

    Signior Baptista, you are happily met.
    [To Pedant] Sir, this is the gentleman I told you of.   20

IV, iv S.D. *booted* (as from travelling)   2 *but* unless   3 *may remember me*
(the Pedant is rehearsing his part)   5 *Pegasus* (common name for an inn,
after the winged horse of classical mythology)   9 *schooled* instructed how
to play his part   11 *throughly* thoroughly   17 *tall* fine   18 S.D. *bare-
headed* (the Pedant doffs his cap to Baptista)   19 *happily* luckily

I pray you, stand good father to me now,
Give me Bianca for my patrimony.
Pedant. Soft, son.
    Sir, by your leave. Having come to Padua
25 To gather in some debts, my son Lucentio
Made me acquainted with a weighty cause
Of love between your daughter and himself.
And — for the good report I hear of you,
And for the love he beareth to your daughter,
30 And she to him — to stay him not too long,
I am content, in a good father's care,
To have him matched. And if you please to like
No worse than I, upon some agreement
Me shall you find ready and willing
35 With one consent to have her so bestowed.
For curious I cannot be with you,
Signior Baptista, of whom I hear so well.
Baptista. Sir, pardon me in what I have to say.
Your plainness and your shortness please me well.
40 Right true it is, your son Lucentio here
Doth love my daughter, and she loveth him —
Or both dissemble deeply their affections.
And therefore if you say no more than this,
That like a father you will deal with him
45 And pass my daughter a sufficient dower,
The match is made and all is done:
Your son shall have my daughter with consent.
Tranio. I thank you, sir. Where then do you know best
We be affied and such assurance ta'en
50 As shall with either part's agreement stand?
Baptista. Not in my house, Lucentio, for you know

36 *curious* overparticular   45 *pass* settle upon   49 *affied* betrothed

Pitchers have ears, and I have many servants.
Besides, old Gremio is heark'ning still,
And happily we might be interrupted.

Tranio. Then at my lodging, an it like you.   55
There doth my father lie, and there this night
We'll pass the business privately and well.
Send for your daughter by your servant here.
My boy shall fetch the scrivener presently.
The worst is this, that at so slender warning   60
You are like to have a thin and slender pittance.

Baptista. It likes me well. Cambio, hie you home
And bid Bianca make her ready straight.
And if you will, tell what hath happenèd:
Lucentio's father is arrived in Padua,   65
And how she's like to be Lucentio's wife.

                                    [*Exit Lucentio.*]

Biondello. I pray the gods she may with all my heart.

                                                    Exit.

Tranio. Dally not with the gods, but get thee gone.
Signior Baptista, shall I lead the way?
Welcome, one mess is like to be your cheer.   70
Come, sir, we will better it in Pisa.

Baptista. I follow you.   *Exeunt.*

   Enter [severally] Lucentio [as Cambio] and Biondello.

Biondello. Cambio!
Lucentio. What sayst thou, Biondello?
Biondello. You saw my master wink and laugh upon you? 75

---

53 *heark'ning still* continually eavesdropping   54 *happily* haply, perchance
55 *an it like you* if you please   56 *lie* lodge   57 *pass* transact   59 *scrivener*
scribe specializing in legal agreements   61 *pittance* portion of food   70
mess dish   *cheer* entertainment

Lucentio. Biondello, what of that?

Biondello. Faith, nothing, but 'has left me here behind to
   expound the meaning or moral of his signs and tokens.

Lucentio. I pray thee, moralize them.

80 *Biondello.* Then thus. Baptista is safe, talking with the de-
   ceiving father of a deceitful son.

Lucentio. And what of him?

Biondello. His daughter is to be brought by you to the
   supper.

85 *Lucentio.* And then?

Biondello. The old priest at Saint Luke's church is at your
   command at all hours.

Lucentio. And what of all this?

Biondello. I cannot tell, except they are busied about a
90   counterfeit assurance. Take you assurance of her, 'cum
   privilegio ad imprimendum solum.' To th' church! Take
   the priest, clerk, and some sufficient honest witnesses.
   If this be not that you look for, I have no more to say,
   But bid Bianca farewell forever and a day.

95 *Lucentio.* Hear'st thou, Biondello?

Biondello. I cannot tarry. I knew a wench married in an
   afternoon as she went to the garden for parsley to stuff
   a rabbit, and so may you, sir, and so adieu, sir. My master
   hath appointed me to go to Saint Luke's, to bid the
100   priest be ready to come against you come with your
   appendix.   *Exit.*

Lucentio. I may and will, if she be so contented.
   She will be pleased, then wherefore should I doubt?

77 *'has* he has   78 *moral* hidden meaning   79 *moralize* explain   90 *assurance* agreement (the betrothal)   *Take you assurance* make yourself sure
90–91 *cum privilegio . . . solum* with sole rights of printing (copyright
formula; with a play on the husband's conjugal rights, exercise of which
will *assure* the marriage)   100 *against you come* in anticipation of your
coming   101 *appendix* adjunct (i.e. bride)

Hap what hap may, I'll roundly go about her.
It shall go hard if Cambio go without her.   *Exit.* 105

Enter Petruchio, Kate, Hortensio, [and Grumio, with   IV, v
    Attendants].

Petruchio. Come on, a God's name, once more toward our
    father's.
  Good Lord, how bright and goodly shines the moon!
Kate. The moon? The sun. It is not moonlight now.
Petruchio. I say it is the moon that shines so bright.
Kate. I know it is the sun that shines so bright.   5
Petruchio. Now by my mother's son, and that's myself,
    It shall be moon or star or what I list,
    Or e'er I journey to your father's house.
    [To Servants] Go on and fetch our horses back again.
    Evermore crossed and crossed, nothing but crossed.   10
Hortensio. *[aside to Kate]* Say as he says or we shall never go.
Kate. Forward, I pray, since we have come so far,
    And be it moon or sun or what you please.
    An if you please to call it a rush-candle,
    Henceforth I vow it shall be so for me.   15
Petruchio. I say it is the moon.
Kate.   I know it is the moon.
Petruchio. Nay, then you lie. It is the blessèd sun.
Kate. Then God be blessed, it is the blessèd sun,
    But sun it is not when you say it is not,
    And the moon changes even as your mind.   20

104 *roundly* straightway *go about her* seek her out IV, v, 1 *a* in 7 *list*
please 8 *Or ere,* before 14 *rush-candle* rush dipped in grease to serve
as candle

What you will have it named, even that it is,
And so it shall be still for Katherine.

Hortensio. Petruchio, go thy ways, the field is won.

Petruchio. Well, forward, forward! Thus the bowl should
    run,
25   And not unluckily against the bias.
But soft, company is coming here.

Enter Vincentio.

[*To Vincentio*] Good morrow, gentle mistress, where
    away?
Tell me, sweet Kate, and tell me truly too,
Hast thou beheld a fresher gentlewoman?
30   Such war of white and red within her cheeks!
What stars do spangle heaven with such beauty
As those two eyes become that heavenly face?
Fair lovely maid, once more good day to thee.
Sweet Kate, embrace her for her beauty's sake.

Hortensio. [*aside*] 'A will make the man mad, to make a
35   woman of him.

Kate. Young budding virgin, fair and fresh and sweet,
Whither away, or where is thy abode?
Happy the parents of so fair a child,
Happier the man whom favorable stars
40   Allots thee for his lovely bedfellow.

Petruchio. Why, how now, Kate, I hope thou art not mad.
This is a man, old, wrinkled, faded, withered,
And not a maiden, as thou sayst he is.

Kate. Pardon, old father, my mistaking eyes

22 *still* always   24 *bowl* ball in game of bowls   25 *unluckily* unsuccess-
fully   *against the bias* contrary to designed course (the *bias* being a weight
in the side of the bowl which enables the bowler to roll it in a curve)
35 *'A* he   44 *father* (respectful term of address to an old man)

That have been so bedazzled with the sun   45
That everything I look on seemeth green.
Now I perceive thou art a reverend father.
Pardon, I pray thee, for my mad mistaking.
Petruchio. Do, good old grandsire, and withal make known
    Which way thou travell'st. If along with us,   50
    We shall be joyful of thy company.
Vincentio. Fair sir, and you my merry mistress,
    That with your strange encounter much amazed me,
    My name is called Vincentio, my dwelling Pisa,
    And bound I am to Padua, there to visit   55
    A son of mine, which long I have not seen.
Petruchio. What is his name?
Vincentio.   Lucentio, gentle sir.
Petruchio. Happily met, the happier for thy son.
    And now by law, as well as reverend age,
    I may entitle thee my loving father.   60
    The sister to my wife, this gentlewoman,
    Thy son by this hath married. Wonder not
    Nor be not grieved. She is of good esteem,
    Her dowry wealthy, and of worthy birth;
    Beside, so qualified as may beseem   65
    The spouse of any noble gentleman.
    Let me embrace with old Vincentio,
    And wander we to see thy honest son,
    Who will of thy arrival be full joyous.
Vincentio. But is this true, or is it else your pleasure,   70
    Like pleasant travellers, to break a jest
    Upon the company you overtake?
Hortensio. I do assure thee, father, so it is.

46 *green* i.e. young   53 *encounter* manner of greeting   62 *by this* by this
time   63 *esteem* reputation   65 *so qualified* having such qualities   71
pleasant merry

Petruchio. Come, go along, and see the truth hereof,
75   For our first merriment hath made thee jealous.
                              Exeunt [all but Hortensio].
Hortensio. Well, Petruchio, this has put me in heart.
    Have to my widow, and if she be froward,
    Then hast thou taught Hortensio to be untoward. *Exit.*

V, i   *Enter Biondello, Lucentio [as Cambio], and Bianca.*
        Gremio is out before [and stands aside].

Biondello. Softly and swiftly, sir, for the priest is ready.
Lucentio. I fly, Biondello — but they may chance to need
    thee at home; therefore leave us.   *Exit [with Bianca].*
Biondello. Nay, faith, I'll see the church a your back, and
5   then come back to my master as soon as I can.   *[Exit.]*
Gremio. I marvel Cambio comes not all this while.

        Enter Petruchio, Kate, Vincentio, [and] Grumio, with
        Attendants.

Petruchio. Sir, here's the door, this is Lucentio's house.
    My father's bears more toward the market-place.
    Thither must I, and here I leave you, sir.
10 *Vincentio.* You shall not choose but drink before you go.
    I think I shall command your welcome here,
    And by all likelihood some cheer is toward.   *Knock.*
Gremio. [advancing] They're busy within; you were best
    knock louder.

75 *jealous* suspicious   77 *Have to* now for   78 *untoward* perverse   V, i s.d.
out before i.e. on stage first (he enters before the others, whom he does
not 'see')   4 *a* on   8 *bears* lies (nautical term)

Pedant [as Vincentio] looks out of the window.

Pedant. What's he that knocks as he would beat down the 15
    gate?

Vincentio. Is Signior Lucentio within, sir?

Pedant. He's within, sir, but not to be spoken withal.

Vincentio. What if a man bring him a hundred pound or
    two, to make merry withal? 20

Pedant. Keep your hundred pounds to yourself. He shall
    need none so long as I live.

Petruchio. Nay, I told you your son was well beloved in
    Padua. Do you hear, sir? To leave frivolous circum-
    stances, I pray you tell Signior Lucentio that his father is 25
    come from Pisa and is here at the door to speak with him.

Pedant. Thou liest. His father is come from Pisa and here
    looking out at the window.

Vincentio. Art thou his father?

Pedant. Ay sir, so his mother says, if I may believe her. 30

Petruchio. *[to Vincentio]* Why how now, gentleman! Why
    this is flat knavery, to take upon you another man's name.

Pedant. Lay hands on the villain. I believe 'a means to cozen
    somebody in this city under my countenance.

Enter Biondello.

Biondello. I have seen them in the church together. God 35
    send 'em good shipping! But who is here? Mine old
    master, Vincentio! Now we are undone and brought to
    nothing.

Vincentio. Come hither, crack-hemp.

---

14 S.D. *looks . . . window* i.e. appears in the tiring-house gallery over the
stage 15 *What* who 18 *withal* with 32 *flat* downright 33 *cozen*
cheat 34 *under my countenance* by posing as me 36 *good shipping* fair
sailing 37 *undone* ruined 39 *crack-hemp* fellow ripe for hanging

40 *Biondello.* I hope I may choose, sir.

Vincentio. Come hither, you rogue. What, have you forgot
me?

Biondello. Forgot you? No sir. I could not forget you, for
I never saw you before in all my life.

45 *Vincentio.* What, you notorious villain, didst thou never
see thy master's father, Vincentio?

Biondello. What, my worshipful old master? Yes, marry,
sir, see where he looks out of the window.

Vincentio. Is't so indeed?   *He beats Biondello.*

50 *Biondello.* Help, help, help! Here's a madman will murder
me.   *[Exit.]*

Pedant. Help, son! Help, Signior Baptista!   *[Exit above.]*

Petruchio. Prithee, Kate, let's stand aside and see the end of
this controversy.   *[They stand aside.]*

*Enter [below] Pedant [as Vincentio] with Servants,
Baptista, [and] Tranio [as Lucentio].*

55 *Tranio.* Sir, what are you that offer to beat my servant?

Vincentio. What am I, sir? Nay, what are you, sir? O im-
mortal gods! O fine villain! A silken doublet, a velvet
hose, a scarlet cloak, and a copatain hat! O I am undone,
I am undone! While I play the good husband at home,

60 my son and my servant spend all at the university.

Tranio. How now, what's the matter?

Baptista. What, is the man lunatic?

Tranio. Sir, you seem a sober ancient gentleman by your
habit, but your words show you a madman. Why sir,

65 what 'cerns it you if I wear pearl and gold? I thank my
good father, I am able to maintain it.

40 *choose* do as I choose   55 *what* who   58 *copatain* high-crowned   59
good husband careful manager   64 *habit* bearing   65 *'cerns* concerns

Vincentio. Thy father! O villain, he is a sailmaker in Bergamo.

Baptista. You mistake, sir, you mistake, sir. Pray, what do you think is his name?   70

Vincentio. His name? As if I knew not his name! I have brought him up ever since he was three years old, and his name is Tranio.

Pedant. Away, away, mad ass! His name is Lucentio, and he is mine only son, and heir to the lands of me, Signior   75 Vincentio.

Vincentio. Lucentio? O he hath murd'red his master! Lay hold on him, I charge you in the Duke's name. O my son, my son! Tell me, thou villain, where is my son Lucentio?   80

Tranio. [*to a Servant*] Call forth an officer.

[*Enter an Officer.*]

Carry this mad knave to the jail. Father Baptista, I charge you see that he be forthcoming.

Vincentio. Carry me to the jail!

Gremio. Stay, officer, he shall not go to prison.   85

Baptista. Talk not, Signior Gremio. I say he shall go to prison.

Gremio. Take heed, Signior Baptista, lest you be conycatched in this business. I dare to swear this is the right Vincentio.   90

Pedant. Swear, if thou dar'st.

Gremio. Nay, I dare not swear it.

Tranio. Then thou wert best say that I am not Lucentio.

Gremio. Yes, I know thee to be Signior Lucentio.

Baptista. Away with the dotard, to the jail with him!   95

83 *forthcoming* i.e. to stand trial   88–89 *cony-catched* duped   93 *wert best* might as well

Enter Biondello, Lucentio, and Bianca.

Vincentio. Thus strangers may be halèd and abused.
　　O monstrous villain!

Biondello. O we are spoiled, and yonder he is. Deny him,
　　forswear him, or else we are all undone.

　　　　　　　　　　　Exeunt Biondello, Tranio, and
　　　　　　　　　　　Pedant as fast as may be.

100 *Lucentio.* Pardon, sweet father.　　　　　*Kneel.*

Vincentio. Lives my sweet son?

Bianca. Pardon, dear father.

Baptista. How hast thou offended? Where is Lucentio?

Lucentio. Here's Lucentio, right son to the right Vincentio,

105　　That have by marriage made thy daughter mine
　　While counterfeit supposes bleared thine eyne.

Gremio. Here's packing, with a witness, to deceive us all!

Vincentio. Where is that damnèd villain Tranio,
　　That faced and braved me in this matter so?

110 *Baptista.* Why, tell me, is not this my Cambio?

Bianca. Cambio is changed into Lucentio.

Lucentio. Love wrought these miracles. Bianca's love
　　Made me exchange my state with Tranio
　　While he did bear my countenance in the town,

115　　And happily I have arrivèd at the last
　　Unto the wishèd haven of my bliss.
　　What Tranio did, myself enforced him to;
　　Then pardon him, sweet father, for my sake.

Vincentio. I'll slit the villain's nose that would have sent

120　　me to the jail.

96 *halèd* hauled about, molested　106 *counterfeit supposes* false assumptions (with an allusion to Gascoigne's play, the *Supposes*) *eyne* eyes 107 *packing* plotting　*with a witness* with a vengeance　114 *bear my countenance* pose as me

Baptista. *[to Lucentio]* But do you hear, sir? Have you married my daughter without asking my good will?

Vincentio. Fear not, Baptista, we will content you, go to. But I will in, to be revenged for this villainy. *Exit.*

Baptista. And I, to sound the depth of this knavery. 125
Exit.

Lucentio. Look not pale, Bianca, thy father will not frown.
Exeunt [Lucentio and Bianca.]

Gremio. My cake is dough, but I'll in among the rest, Out of hope of all but my share of the feast. *[Exit.]*

Kate. *[advancing]* Husband, let's follow, to see the end of this ado. 130

Petruchio. First kiss me, Kate, and we will.

Kate. What, in the midst of the street?

Petruchio. What, art thou ashamed of me?

Kate. No sir, God forbid, but ashamed to kiss.

Petruchio. Why, then let's home again. *[to Grumio]* Come, sirrah, let's away. 135

Kate. Nay, I will give thee a kiss. Now pray thee, love, stay.

Petruchio. Is not this well? Come, my sweet Kate. Better once than never, for never too late. *Exeunt.*

123 *go to* (expression of impatience)   127 *My cake is dough* i.e. my hopes are dashed (proverbial)   138 *Better . . . late* i.e. better late than never (proverbial)   *once* at one time or another

V, ii   *Enter Baptista, Vincentio, Gremio, the Pedant, Lucentio,*
          and Bianca; Tranio, Biondello, [and] Grumio; [Pe-
          truchio, Kate, Hortensio,] and Widow; the Serving-
          men with Tranio bringing in a banquet.

    Lucentio. At last, though long, our jarring notes agree,
          And time it is, when raging war is done,
          To smile at 'scapes and perils overblown.
          My fair Bianca, bid my father welcome
5   While I with self-same kindness welcome thine.
          Brother Petruchio, sister Katherina,
          And thou, Hortensio, with thy loving widow,
          Feast with the best and welcome to my house.
          My banquet is to close our stomachs up
10   After our great good cheer. Pray you, sit down,
          For now we sit to chat as well as eat.
                                        [They sit at table.]
    Petruchio. Nothing but sit and sit, and eat and eat!
    Baptista. Padua affords this kindness, son Petruchio.
    Petruchio. Padua affords nothing but what is kind.
15 *Hortensio.* For both our sakes I would that word were true.
    Petruchio. Now, for my life, Hortensio fears his widow.
    Widow. Then never trust me if I be afeard.
    Petruchio. You are very sensible, and yet you miss my
          sense:
          I mean Hortensio is afeard of you.
20 *Widow.* He that is giddy thinks the world turns round.
    Petruchio. Roundly replied.
    Kate.   Mistress, how mean you that?

V, ii S.D. *bringing in* i.e. carrying onstage   *banquet* dessert (sweetmeats,
fruit, and wine)   1 *long* after a long time   10 *After . . . cheer* (Lucentio's
banquet apparently follows a bridal feast given by Baptista)   16 *fears* is
afraid of (the Widow quibbles on 'frightens')   17 *afeard* frightened (Petruchio quibbles on 'suspicious')   21 *Roundly* straightforwardly

Widow. Thus I conceive by him.

Petruchio. Conceives by me? How likes Hortensio that?

Hortensio. My widow says, thus she conceives her tale.

Petruchio. Very well mended. Kiss him for that, good
    widow.   25

Kate. 'He that is giddy thinks the world turns round' —
    I pray you, tell me what you meant by that.

Widow. Your husband, being troubled with a shrow,
    Measures my husband's sorrow by his woe —
    And now you know my meaning.   30

Kate. A very mean meaning.

Widow.   Right, I mean you.

Kate. And I am mean indeed, respecting you.

Petruchio. To her, Kate!

Hortensio. To her, widow!

Petruchio. A hundred marks, my Kate does put her down.   35

Hortensio. That's my office.

Petruchio. Spoke like an officer — ha' to thee, lad.

                          Drinks to Hortensio.

Baptista. How likes Gremio these quick-witted folks?

Gremio. Believe me, sir, they butt together well.

Bianca. Head and butt! An hasty-witted body   40
    Would say your head and butt were head and horn.

Vincentio. Ay, mistress bride, hath that awakened you?

Bianca. Ay, but not frighted me; therefore I'll sleep again.

Petruchio. Nay, that you shall not; since you have begun,
    Have at you for a bitter jest or two.   45

---

22 *conceive by* am inspired by (Petruchio quibbles on 'become pregnant
by')   24 *conceives* devises   29 *Measures* judges   31 *mean* contemptible
(the Widow quibbles on 'have in mind,' and Kate then quibbles on 'mod-
erate,' i.e. in shrewishness)   32 *respecting* compared with   35 *put her down*
defeat her (Hortensio quibbles bawdily)   41 *Would say . . . horn* (meaning
uncertain; *horn* may involve the common Elizabethan joke about cuckoldry
or a play on 'phallus' or both)   45 *Have . . . for* let's exchange   *bitter* sharp

Bianca. Am I your bird? I mean to shift my bush,
    And then pursue me as you draw your bow.
    You are welcome all.

                    Exit Bianca [with Kate and Widow].

Petruchio. She hath prevented me. Here, Signior Tranio,
50   This bird you aimed at, though you hit her not.
    Therefore a health to all that shot and missed.

Tranio. O sir, Lucentio slipped me, like his greyhound,
    Which runs himself and catches for his master.

Petruchio. A good swift simile but something currish.

55 *Tranio.* 'Tis well, sir, that you hunted for yourself;
    'Tis thought your deer does hold you at a bay.

Baptista. O, O, Petruchio! Tranio hits you now.

Lucentio. I thank thee for that gird, good Tranio.

Hortensio. Confess, confess, hath he not hit you here?

60 *Petruchio.* 'A has a little galled me, I confess,
    And as the jest did glance away from me,
    'Tis ten to one it maimed you two outright.

Baptista. Now, in good sadness, son Petruchio,
    I think thou hast the veriest shrew of all.

65 *Petruchio.* Well, I say no. And therefore, for assurance,
    Let's each one send unto his wife,
    And he whose wife is most obedient,
    To come at first when he doth send for her,
    Shall win the wager which we will propose.

Hortensio. Content. What's the wager?

70 *Lucentio.*   Twenty crowns.

Petruchio. Twenty crowns?

---

49 *prevented* forestalled *Signior* (ironically) 52 *slipped* unleashed 56 *deer* (punning on 'dear') *hold you at a bay* (like a hunted animal that turns to fight and thus keeps the hounds baying at a distance) 58 *gird* taunt 60 *galled* annoyed 63 *sadness* seriousness 64 *veriest* most perfect 65 *assurance* proof

I'll venture so much of my hawk or hound,
But twenty times so much upon my wife.
Lucentio. A hundred then.
Hortensio.   Content.
Petruchio.   A match, 'tis done.
Hortensio. Who shall begin?   75
Lucentio. That will I.
　Go, Biondello, bid your mistress come to me.
Biondello. I go.   *Exit.*
Baptista. Son, I'll be your half, Bianca comes.
Lucentio. I'll have no halves; I'll bear it all myself.   80

Enter Biondello.

How now, what news?
Biondello. Sir, my mistress sends you word
　That she is busy and she cannot come.
Petruchio. How? 'She's busy and she cannot come'?
　Is that an answer?
Gremio.   Ay, and a kind one too.   85
　Pray God, sir, your wife send you not a worse.
Petruchio. I hope better.
Hortensio. Sirrah Biondello, go and entreat my wife to
　come to me forthwith.   *Exit Biondello.*
Petruchio. O ho, 'entreat her'! Nay, then she must needs 90
　come.
Hortensio. I am afraid, sir, do what you can

Enter Biondello.

Yours will not be entreated. — Now, where's my wife?
Biondello. She says you have some goodly jest in hand.

72 *of* on   74 *match* bet   79 *be your half* take half your bet that   89 *forthwith* immediately

95   She will not come. She bids you come to her.
   Petruchio. Worse and worse, 'she will not come'!
     O vile, intolerable, not to be endured!
     Sirrah Grumio, go to your mistress,
     Say I command her come to me.   *Exit [Grumio].*
100 *Hortensio.* I know her answer.
   Petruchio. What?
   Hortensio. She will not.
   Petruchio. The fouler fortune mine, and there an end.

                Enter Kate [with Grumio].

   Baptista. Now, by my halidom, here comes Katherina!
105 *Kate.* What is your will, sir, that you send for me?
   Petruchio. Where is your sister and Hortensio's wife?
   Kate. They sit conferring by the parlor fire.
   Petruchio. Go fetch them hither. If they deny to come,
     Swinge me them soundly forth unto their husbands.
110   Away, I say, and bring them hither straight.
                              [Exit Kate.]
   Lucentio. Here is a wonder, if you talk of a wonder.
   Hortensio. And so it is. I wonder what it bodes.
   Petruchio. Marry, peace it bodes, and love, and quiet life,
     An awful rule and right supremacy,
115   And, to be short, what not that's sweet and happy.
   Baptista. Now fair befall thee, good Petruchio.
     The wager thou hast won, and I will add
     Unto their losses twenty thousand crowns,
     Another dowry to another daughter,
120   For she is changed as she had never been.
   Petruchio. Nay, I will win my wager better yet

   104 *by my halidom* bless my soul (originally an oath by a sacred relic)
   109 *Swinge* whip   114 *awful* commanding respect   116 *fair befall thee*
   good luck to you

And show more sign of her obedience,
Her new-built virtue and obedience.

Enter Kate, Bianca, and Widow.

See where she comes and brings your froward wives
As prisoners to her womanly persuasion.   125
Katherine, that cap of yours becomes you not.
Off with that bauble, throw it under foot. *[She obeys.]*
Widow. Lord, let me never have a cause to sigh
    Till I be brought to such a silly pass.
Bianca. Fie, what a foolish duty call you this?   130
Lucentio. I would your duty were as foolish too.
    The wisdom of your duty, fair Bianca,
    Hath cost me a hundred crowns since suppertime.
Bianca. The more fool you for laying on my duty.
Petruchio. Katherine, I charge thee, tell these headstrong
        women   135
    What duty they do owe their lords and husbands.
Widow. Come, come, you're mocking; we will have no
        telling.
Petruchio. Come on, I say, and first begin with her.
Widow. She shall not.
Petruchio. I say she shall — and first begin with her.   140
Kate. Fie, fie, unknit that threat'ning unkind brow
    And dart not scornful glances from those eyes
    To wound thy lord, thy king, thy governor.
    It blots thy beauty as frosts do bite the meads,
    Confounds thy fame as whirlwinds shake fair buds,   145
    And in no sense is meet or amiable.
    A woman moved is like a fountain troubled,

129 *pass* predicament 134 *laying* betting 141 *unkind* unamiable 143
governor ruler 145 *Confounds thy fame* spoils your good name 147 *moved*
angry

Muddy, ill-seeming, thick, bereft of beauty,
And while it is so, none so dry or thirsty
150 Will deign to sip or touch one drop of it.
Thy husband is thy lord, thy life, thy keeper,
Thy head, thy sovereign; one that cares for thee
And for thy maintenance; commits his body
To painful labor both by sea and land,
155 To watch the night in storms, the day in cold,
Whilst thou li'st warm at home, secure and safe;
And craves no other tribute at thy hands
But love, fair looks, and true obedience —
Too little payment for so great a debt.
160 Such duty as the subject owes the prince,
Even such a woman oweth to her husband;
And when she is froward, peevish, sullen, sour,
And not obedient to his honest will,
What is she but a foul contending rebel
165 And graceless traitor to her loving lord?
I am ashamed that women are so simple
To offer war where they should kneel for peace,
Or seek for rule, supremacy, and sway,
When they are bound to serve, love, and obey.
170 Why are our bodies soft and weak and smooth,
Unapt to toil and trouble in the world,
But that our soft conditions and our hearts
Should well agree with our external parts?
Come, come, you froward and unable worms,
175 My mind hath been as big as one of yours,
My heart as great, my reason haply more,

152 *head* commander   160 *prince* monarch   162 *peevish* refractory, self-willed   166 *simple* foolish   171 *Unapt to* unsuited for   172 *conditions* qualities   174 *unable* feeble   *worms* i.e. pitiful creatures   175 *big* haughty

To bandy word for word and frown for frown.
But now I see our lances are but straws,
Our strength as weak, our weakness past compare,
That seeming to be most which we indeed least are.   180
Then vail your stomachs, for it is no boot,
And place your hands below your husband's foot,
In token of which duty, if he please,
My hand is ready, may it do him ease.

Petruchio. Why, there's a wench! Come on and kiss me,
    Kate!   185
Lucentio. Well, go thy ways, old lad, for thou shalt ha't.
Vincentio. 'Tis a good hearing when children are toward.
Lucentio. But a harsh hearing when women are froward.
Petruchio. Come, Kate, we'll to bed.
    We three are married, but you two are sped.   190
    [To Lucentio] 'Twas I won the wager, though you hit the
        white,
    And being a winner, God give you good night.
                              Exit Petruchio [with Kate].
Hortensio. Now, go thy ways, thou hast tamed a curst
    shrow.
Lucentio. 'Tis a wonder, by your leave, she will be tamèd so.
                                              [Exeunt.]

177 *bandy* exchange (as in hitting a tennis ball back and forth)   181 *vail
your stomachs* curb your willfulness   *no boot* no use   184 *may it* if it may
187 *a good hearing* i.e. good news   *toward* docile   190 *sped* done for
(through having disobedient wives)   191 *white* bull's-eye (playing on
Bianca, white)

Appendix: The History and Text of the Play

The history of *The Taming of the Shrew* is complicated by the existence of an anonymous play entitled *The Taming of a Shrew*, printed in 1594. This was once thought to be a source of Shakespeare's *Shrew* but is now usually assumed to be a "bad" quarto, or memorial reconstruction. Because of the puzzling fact that, despite a rough agreement in plot and characterization, the scene and most of the names of *A Shrew* differ radically from those of *The Shrew*, certain textual scholars, notably G. I. Duthie (in *The Review of English Studies*, 1943), have postulated the existence of a lost Shrew play which served as a source of *The Shrew* and of which *A Shrew* is a bad quarto. But others, notably Peter Alexander (in *The Times Literary Supplement*, September 16, 1926), have assumed that *A Shrew* is simply a bad quarto of *The Shrew*, although of an unusual type. If the latter theory is correct, *A Shrew* must represent, not an attempt to reconstruct Shakespeare's play literally, but an attempt to write a play, in certain respects intentionally different from Shakespeare's, on the basis of a general knowledge, held in memory, of *The Taming of the Shrew*. The reporters responsible for *A Shrew* could not have "forgotten" Petruchio's name or that the scene was laid in Italy—but they might, for reasons that remain obscure, intentionally have altered Petruchio's name to Ferando and the scene from Italy to Greece. A reader interested in comparing the two Shrew plays will find *A Shrew* reprinted in Geoffrey Bullough's *Narrative and Dramatic Sources of Shakespeare*, vol. I (1957).

Performance by Pembroke's Men, a company active in 1592–93, is recorded on the title-page of *A Shrew*. The reference may be to either *A Shrew* or *The Shrew*. If it is to *The Shrew*, then the publisher of *A Shrew*, like the publisher of the bad quarto of *Romeo and Juliet* (1597), presumably referred, in the interests of selling his book, to the well-known company that had produced a generally similar but better play of essentially the same title. (Since for purposes of copyright *A Shrew* and *The Shrew* were regarded as one, it is clear that—contrary to modern usage—no particular significance was attached to the small variation in title; such apparent lack of discrimination is perhaps more readily understandable at a time when *The Shrew* was not yet in print.) Thus *The Shrew*, if it was originally a Pembroke's play, may be dated 1593 or earlier—

probably 1593, in view of the maturity of its characterization in comparison with the characterization of other of Shakespeare's plays usually dated in or before that year. It may be added that a date of 1593 for *The Shrew* is consistent with Peter Short's registration of copyright early in May of 1594 and with his consequent publication of *A Shrew* sometime during that year. In June of 1594, according to Philip Henslowe's *Diary*, a play called *The Taming of a Shrew* was performed in the theatre at Newington Butts, about a mile to the south of London Bridge, where the Admiral's Men and the Chamberlain's Men were then playing, whether separately or in combination is not clear. Since *The Shrew* was later the property of Shakespeare's company, we may infer that the play recorded by Henslowe was probably Shakespeare's *Shrew* and the performing company probably the Chamberlain's Men, who, organized early in 1594, may have taken it over from the disbanded Pembroke's Men. *The Shrew* is not mentioned by Francis Meres in *Palladis Tamia* (1598), but since Meres also failed to name *Henry VI* it is clear that he was not proposing a complete list of Shakespeare's plays.

The Shrew was first printed in the Shakespeare folio of 1623, next in a quarto of 1631. The title-page of the quarto edition alludes to performance by the King's Men, as Shakespeare's company was styled after 1603, at both the Globe and the Blackfriars. The same company, according to Sir Henry Herbert, gave a court performance of *The Shrew* ("liked") before King Charles and Queen Henrietta in November of 1633, followed shortly by a performance of *The Woman's Prize, or The Tamer Tamed* ("very well liked") before the same audience. In this sequel to Shakespeare's play, by John Fletcher, Kate has died and a second wife gets the better of Petruchio.

For nearly two centuries after the Restoration Shakespeare's *Shrew* was neglected in favor of "improved" versions. In 1667 the comedian John Lacy made an adaptation called *Sauny the Scot*, in which the induction was eliminated and his own part of Sauny (Grumio) much magnified and embellished with a sort of Scots accent. Pepys could not understand the words and pronounced it "a silly play." In 1716 the Sly material was worked up by rival dramatists, Charles Johnson and Christopher Bullock, as two farces each entitled *The Cobbler of Preston*. In 1756 Garrick adapted the main plot of Shakespeare's play as a farce called *Catherine and*

Petruchio, in which induction and subplot are eliminated (Bianca being already married to Hortensio), Kate breaks a lute on the head of a real music-master, and Baptista is substituted for Vincentio in the scene corresponding to IV, v. This version continued to be produced as an afterpiece for over a century and still occasionally influences performances of the full-length *Shrew.* In 1844 J. R. Planché, encouraged by Ben Webster, finally returned to Shakespeare's version, induction and all, and in 1887 Augustin Daly mounted a much-praised production with Ada Rehan as Katherine and John Drew as Petruchio. Daly rearranged the order of scenes to accommodate his scenery, but he used the induction and strengthened the new tradition of producing Shakespeare instead of Garrick. Since then *The Shrew* has had a continual stage history, nowadays generally being produced with the subplot intact. Sometimes the induction is omitted, and sometimes when it is used Sly remains on stage throughout the play proper and is carried off asleep at the end, as in *The Taming of a Shrew.* In 1948 *The Shrew* was adapted as the successful musical comedy *Kiss Me Kate,* with music and lyrics by Cole Porter.

The present edition of *The Taming of the Shrew* follows the text of the Shakespeare folio of 1623, thought by Sir Walter Greg (*The Shakespeare First Folio,* 1955) to have been printed from Shakespeare's "foul papers"—that is, from a manuscript which was the author's last working draft before preparation of a promptbook designed to regulate performances. F provides a fairly good text, though in a few places probably corrupt beyond hope of successful emendation. The present text is a conservative one, incorporating for the most part only emendations that conform to the consensus of modern editorial opinion. These are listed below in italic type, together with the corresponding readings of F in roman.

Ind., i s.d. *Christophero Sly* (in F at end of s.d.) 9–10 *thirdborough* Head-borough 15 *Breathe* Brach 20, 28 *1. Huntsman* Hunts. 81 *A Player* 2. Player 87 *A Player* Sincklo 99 *A Player* Plai.

Ind., ii, 2 *lordship* Lord 25 *it is* is it 71 *Christophero* Christopher 91 *Greet* Greece 134 *play it. Is not* play, it is not

I, i, 13 *Vincentio* Vincentio's 47 s.d. *suitor* sister 128 *take her* take 240 *your* you 244 s.d. *speak* speakes

I, ii, 18 *masters* mistris 71 *she* she is 118 *me and other* me. Other
169 *help me* helpe one 210 *ours* yours 262 *feat* seeke

II, i, 3 *gawds* goods 8 *charge thee* charge 75–76 *wooing. Neighbor,
this* wooing neighbors: this 78 *unto you* vnto 168 *I will* Ile S.D.
(in F after 167) 180 S.D. (in F after 181) 332 *in* me

III, i, 46 (F heads line *Luc.*) 49 *Bianca* (F omits) 50 *Lucentio*
Bian. 52 *Bianca* Hort. 79 *change* charge *odd* old 80 *Messenger*
Nicke

III, ii, 29 *of thy* of 30 *master, old* master, 53 *swayed* Waid
124 *sir, to* sir, 126 *As I* As

IV, i, 10 S.D. *a Servant* (in F in 167 s.d.) 11 *is't* is 37 *thou wilt* wilt
thou 126 *Food, food, food, food* Soud, soud, soud, soud 167
S.D. *Enter Curtis* Enter Curtis a Seruant (in F after 168)

IV, ii, 4 *Hortensio* Luc. 6, 8 *Lucentio* Hor. 13 *none* me 31 *her*
them 63 *mercatante* Marcantant 71 *Take in* Take me (F heads
line *Par.*)

IV, iii, 81 *is a* is 88 *like a* like 178 *account'st* accountedst

IV, iv S.D. *booted and* (in F in 18 s.d.) 1 *Sir* Sirs 6 *Tranio* (in F
heads 5) 18 S.D. *Pedant bare-headed* Pedant booted and bare
headed 19 (F heads line *Tra.*) 68 (after this line F adds *Enter
Peter*) 89 *except* expect

IV, v, 18 *is* in 22 *still* so 35 *a* the 37 *where* whether 77 *she be*
she

V, i, 5 *master* mistris 27 *Pisa* Padua 46 *master's* Mistris 47 *my*
my old

V, ii, 2 *done* come 45 *bitter* better 65 *for* sir 133 *a* fiue

Details of the
Pelican Shakespeare and
other Penguin series
follow.

THE PELICAN SHAKESPEARE

General Editor: Alfred Harbage

Tragedies

Edited by Maynard Mack	ANTONY AND CLEOPATRA
Harry Levin	CORIOLANUS
Willard Farnham	HAMLET
S. F. Johnson	JULIUS CAESAR
Alfred Harbage	KING LEAR
Alfred Harbage	MACBETH
Gerald E. Bentley	OTHELLO
John E. Hankins	ROMEO AND JULIET
Charlton Hinman	TIMON OF ATHENS★

Comedies

Jonas Barish	ALL'S WELL THAT ENDS WELL★
Ralph Sargent	AS YOU LIKE IT
Paul A. Jorgensen	THE COMEDY OF ERRORS
Robert B. Heilman	CYMBELINE★
Alfred Harbage	LOVE'S LABOR'S LOST
R. C. Bald	MEASURE FOR MEASURE
Brents Stirling	THE MERCHANT OF VENICE
Fredson T. Bowers	THE MERRY WIVES OF WINDSOR
Madeleine Doran	A MIDSUMMER NIGHT'S DREAM
Josephine Waters Bennett	MUCH ADO ABOUT NOTHING
Richard Hosley	THE TAMING OF THE SHREW
Northrop Frye	THE TEMPEST
Virgil Whitaker	TROILUS AND CRESSIDA
Charles Prouty	TWELFTH NIGHT
Berners Jackson	TWO GENTLEMEN OF VERONA★
Baldwin Maxwell	THE WINTER'S TALE

Histories and Poems

M. A. Shaaber	HENRY IV, PART I
Allan Chester	HENRY IV, PART II
Louis B. Wright and V. Freund	HENRY V
Irving Ribner	KING JOHN
Matthew Black	RICHARD II
G. Blakemore Evans	RICHARD III
Douglas Bush	THE SONNETS

★*In preparation*

PLAYS BY BERNARD SHAW

*The following plays are published
in Penguin editions. Each play has the
complete text and the
author's preface*

THE PELICAN GUIDE TO
ENGLISH LITERATURE

EDITED BY BORIS FORD

What this work sets out to offer is a guide to the history and traditions of English Literature, a contour-map of the literary scene. It attempts, that is, to draw up an ordered account of literature that is concerned, first and foremost, with value for the present, and this as a direct encouragement to people to read for themselves.

Each volume sets out to present the reader with four kinds of related material:

1. An account of the social context of literature in each period.
2. A literary survey of the period.
3. Detailed studies of some of the chief writers and works in the period.
4. An Appendix of essential facts for reference purposes.

The *Guide* consists of seven volumes, as follows:

The Age of Chaucer
The Age of Shakespeare
From Donne to Marvell
From Dryden to Johnson
From Blake to Byron
From Dickens to Hardy
The Modern Age